THE BRAND STRATEGY CANVAS

A ONE-PAGE GUIDE FOR STARTUPS

Patrick Woods

Apress®

The Brand Strategy Canvas: A One-Page Guide for Startups

Patrick Woods
San Francisco, CA, USA

ISBN-13 (pbk): 978-1-4842-5158-4   ISBN-13 (electronic): 978-1-4842-5159-1
https://doi.org/10.1007/978-1-4842-5159-1

Copyright © 2020 by Patrick Woods

This work is subject to copyright. All rights are reserved by the Publisher, whether the whole or part of the material is concerned, specifically the rights of translation, reprinting, reuse of illustrations, recitation, broadcasting, reproduction on microfilms or in any other physical way, and transmission or information storage and retrieval, electronic adaptation, computer software, or by similar or dissimilar methodology now known or hereafter developed.

Trademarked names, logos, and images may appear in this book. Rather than use a trademark symbol with every occurrence of a trademarked name, logo, or image we use the names, logos, and images only in an editorial fashion and to the benefit of the trademark owner, with no intention of infringement of the trademark.

The use in this publication of trade names, trademarks, service marks, and similar terms, even if they are not identified as such, is not to be taken as an expression of opinion as to whether or not they are subject to proprietary rights.

While the advice and information in this book are believed to be true and accurate at the date of publication, neither the authors nor the editors nor the publisher can accept any legal responsibility for any errors or omissions that may be made. The publisher makes no warranty, express or implied, with respect to the material contained herein.

> Managing Director, Apress Media LLC: Welmoed Spahr
> Acquisitions Editor: Shiva Ramachandran
> Development Editor: Rita Fernando
> Coordinating Editor: Rita Fernando

Cover designed by eStudioCalamar

Distributed to the book trade worldwide by Springer Science+Business Media New York, 233 Spring Street, 6th Floor, New York, NY 10013. Phone 1-800-SPRINGER, fax (201) 348-4505, e-mail orders-ny@springer-sbm.com, or visit www.springeronline.com. Apress Media, LLC is a California LLC and the sole member (owner) is Springer Science + Business Media Finance Inc (SSBM Finance Inc). SSBM Finance Inc is a **Delaware** corporation.

For information on translations, please e-mail rights@apress.com, or visit http://www.apress.com/rights-permissions.

Apress titles may be purchased in bulk for academic, corporate, or promotional use. eBook versions and licenses are also available for most titles. For more information, reference our Print and eBook Bulk Sales web page at http://www.apress.com/bulk-sales.

Any source code or other supplementary material referenced by the author in this book is available to readers on GitHub via the book's product page, located at www.apress.com/9781484251584. For more detailed information, please visit http://www.apress.com/source-code.

Printed on acid-free paper

This book is dedicated to Founders.

Contents

About the Author vii
Acknowledgments ix
Introduction xi

Chapter 1: Getting Started with the Brand Strategy Canvas 1
Chapter 2: Overview of the Brand Strategy Canvas 13
Chapter 3: Market Opportunity 29
Chapter 4: Rational and Emotional Benefits 49
Chapter 5: Brand Positioning 67
Chapter 6: Defining Your Brand Values 87
Chapter 7: Creating a Brand Personality 95
Chapter 8: Drafting Key Messages 103
Chapter 9: Completing Your Canvas 113
Appendix A: Brand Strategy Canvas Template 119

Index 121

About the Author

Patrick Woods is a writer and fencer living in San Francisco, CA. He is the founder of the developer relations consultancy DeveloperMode and founder and CEO of Orbit, a platform for building and managing developer relationships.

Prior to Orbit, he led Customer Success at Figure Eight and Keen IO, and before that, launched the startup-focused team at the ad agency Archer Malmo, building brands and go-to market plans for early-stage companies.

He has delivered presentations at SxSW, Techstars, and various startup accelerators and incubators around the United States. You can follow him on Twitter @patrickjwoods.

Acknowledgments

First, I say Thank You to all the founders out there, whose tenacity and innovation have inspired this work. I hope in some small way this book helps you make the impact you're driving toward.

The concepts behind the Brand Strategy Canvas were developed during my time at the advertising powerhouse Archer Malmo, and without the support and creativity and partners Gary Backaus and Russ Williams, the Canvas wouldn't exist. The Canvas itself was developed in close conjunction with my two favorite writers Justin Dobbs and Dan Price, both of whom contributed considerably to the structure and intention built into the framework.

Dan and I have given many presentations on the Brand Strategy Canvas over the years, so a special thanks goes to him for the ongoing development of refinement of the ideas you'll find here.

Thanks to Dustin Larimer and Keith Casey for using and recommending the Canvas to people in their network and encouraging me to refine and publish the ideas found in this book.

I'd also like to thank the many friends who provided feedback on early drafts of this manuscript, including Josh Dzielak, Eric Mathews, Ankur Patel, Chuck Thomas, Scott Finney, Virag Reti, Fiona Co, and Mike Hoffmeyer.

Finally, I'm eternally grateful to my wife and partner in adventure, Kirby Wallace, who has provided more than her fair share of copy edits, emotional support, and inspiration along the way.

Introduction

Thanks to platforms like AWS, simplified billing tools, and powerful APIs, it's easier than ever to launch a startup. In fact, in 2018, more than 34,000 venture deals were completed worldwide, and of those, 20,250 were angel and seed-stage transactions—the most active year on record, across the board.[1]

For consumers, this trend is great, since it means they have tons of alternatives to choose from. **But for founders, the ease of starting up simply means more competition.** How can founders compete, and survive?

Thanks to these new tools and technologies, almost anyone can build a *product*. But building a *brand*? It's just as hard as ever.

- And yet, a strong brand is perhaps a company's most defensible intellectual property.

The competition can't copy it, and a clear strategy will ensure consistent and powerful messaging to a high-value audience.

Every founder has to do it, but they don't teach it in school, so how do founders get started? Online guides are too high level to be helpful, and on top of that, the vocabulary of the brand is enigmatic and inconsistent, making it difficult to share ideas and best practices.

Compared to the more objective and data-driven aspects of building a startup, it's no wonder branding seems like a dark art to many founders.

To make matters worse, google "startup branding," and you'll find checklists and ten-step plans that'll tell you to "have a logo" and "be consistent."

Thanks.

- Founders don't need the same old tips and tricks. They need useful tools for building a meaningful brand.

---

[1] https://news.crunchbase.com/news/q4-2018-closes-out-a-record-year-for-the-global-vc-market/

Introduction

In this book that takes the best from ad agency world and the startup trenches, we'll move past what to do about your brand and focus on *how* to actually do it from day 1, equipping your team with actionable brand heuristics they can apply every day.

We'll explore quick-hit methods for jump-starting your strategy creation process that you can start using today, and for those so inclined, we'll dive deep into the concepts of the brand development process.

We'll chart your brand strategy on a single sheet of paper, and we'll look at lots of real-world examples along the way.

In Chapter 1, we'll explore fundamental ideas about branding for startups. What's the difference between strategy and execution, and why does that matter for you?

In Chapter 2, we'll take a high-level look at the Brand Strategy Canvas, a tool I created to help founders actually do branding on a single page. To get started, we'll look at the big picture to see how all the pieces of the canvas fit together, before walking through each section in detail.

Chapter 3 will kick off our deep dive with the Market Opportunity. The first three boxes on the canvas are foundational to the existence of your startup, and key insights about your audience, competition, and product lead to a strong strategy.

Chapter 4 is all about features and benefits. Sounds simple, but once you understand the continuum from feature to rational benefit to emotional benefit, you'll be able to unlock key parts of your brand strategy that will lead to great web site copy, killer campaigns, and, in general, strong messaging.

Chapter 5 gets to the heart of your brand. The positioning statement is a tested tool for succinctly capturing your strategy. It's the foundation and inspiration for all brand execution. Getting it right is tough, but the struggle is worth it.

Chapter 6 explores your startup's values to help ensure you deliver your messaging authentically.

Chapter 7 explores how personality will guide the tone and voice of your brand and provide further opportunities for competitive differentiation.

Chapter 8 delves into your startup's key messages, which is where your strategy becomes actionable. While much of your strategy is internal to your team, your key messages will inform everything from web site copy to press releases to what you say in customer support emails.

Finally, Chapter 9 walks through how each tool from the prior chapters can be applied in the real world and offers lots of best practices for nailing your brand strategy the first time.

Whether you're picking out the highlights from each chapter to spark momentum for your current strategy or digging deep into strategy with your team, you'll walk away armed with ideas and insights that will bring clarity and focus to your strategy and impact to your execution.

CHAPTER 1

Getting Started with the Brand Strategy Canvas
Foundations and Key Concepts

> "I find that most people know what a story is until they sit down to write one."
>
> —Flannery O'Connor, American novelist

Have you ever experienced the overwhelming vastness of a blank page? Maybe it was in a creative writing course in college or maybe just for your company blog. And even though you've *read* lots of blog posts and plenty of books, the words just didn't seem to flow when you sit down to right.

It seems like the two activities, reading and writing, would be closely related. That experience with one would lead to more abilities with the other. But it turns out that, though they're similar, one doesn't necessarily lead to the other.

© Patrick Woods 2020
P. Woods, *The Brand Strategy Canvas*,
https://doi.org/10.1007/978-1-4842-5159-1_1

Similarly, just because we eat food every day doesn't mean we understand how the body turns that food into energy.

In my mentoring and office hours with startups, I've noticed time and again that founders make a similar assumption that experiencing lots of brands will make them experts at *creating* brands. But that's just as dangerous as thinking the reading stories will give you the superpowers to write like an expert author.

To be sure, as a writer, I can tell you that intentional reading is definitely part of honing the craft of writing, but reading *Harry Potter* won't make you J.K. Rowling.

When it comes to brand building, it's easy for founders to lull themselves into the comforting idea that branding will be simple and straightforward, especially when compared to writing powerful code. But as we'll see, this fallacy will only result in pain and frustration.

To make matters worse, most of the advice about brand building focuses on global companies or highly successful later-stage startups, rather than providing tangible steps for early-stage companies.

Starbucks is a perennial favorite in branding books and presentations, as are Airbnb and Dropbox. Sure, we can learn lessons from those giants, but it can be really hard to translate their experiences, with million-dollar budgets, massive teams, and tons of customers, into actionable steps for startup founders.

There's a principle at work here that I call the **baby pigeon problem.**

If you've walked around any large city, you've no doubt seen pigeons walking around everywhere. They're ubiquitous, and they're not really scared of you.

But have you ever seen a *baby* pigeon? I've lived in San Francisco for many years, and have visited cities around the globe, and have never seen a baby pigeon in the streets or in the parks. Where do they come from? How do they grow into the grumpy pigeons hobbling around underfoot?

Here's the thing: almost all of the brand books and marketing experts teach the lessons of adult pigeons—the large companies that are already massively successful. Those lessons are interesting, but they require a lot of translation to be useful for founders at the early stages.

Not to worry, though. I'm here to talk to you about tools and tactics you'll need to start from a place of strength, and maybe someday grow into a big mean grumpy pigeon yourself.

What Is Strategy?

This book is about *strategy*. But most branding advice is centered on *execution*. What's the difference and why does it matter?

You might have noticed that the term "strategy" often gets thrown around a lot by people wanting to sound significant. In fact, strategy often feels like nothing more than a code word for "important." "We need to hire a strategy consultant to craft a strategic plan with strategic thinking." It's also used heavily in the context of military history and grand strategy, describing the movements of armies and the fates of nations.

In that light, strategy probably seems overwhelming and, ultimately, not helpful for a startup founder. But the truth is that a strategy is simply a set of choices you make to focus your time, energy, and effort on a specific outcome.

Time and money are both limited resources, so you naturally have to choose to do some things rather than others. Whether you realize it or not, those kinds of decisions are all strategic in nature. But how do you *do* strategy?

The Kernel of Good Strategy

In his book, *Good Strategy/Bad Strategy: The Difference and Why It Matters*,[1] professor and consultant Richard Rumelt describes the three aspects every good strategy involves:

- A diagnosis
- A guiding policy
- A set of coherent actions

The **diagnosis** describes the nature of the challenge and simplifies the massive complexity by distilling the situation down to its critical parts. The process of working through the Brand Strategy Canvas will help you clarify and communicate your diagnosis.

Your **guiding policy** captures and communicates your approach to addressing the challenges described in your diagnosis. As you make choices throughout the canvas, you'll begin to create things like a positioning statement and a message map that will help direct your team's efforts.

The third part of a good strategy is a **set of coherent actions** that will bring the guiding policy to life. Together, these coordinated actions will provide clear actions for you and your team to implement on a daily basis in service of overcoming the diagnosis and applying the guiding policy.

---

[1] Crown Business, 2011

By the end of the book, you will have diagnosed your specific brand-related challenges, created a set of tools to address those challenges, and set forth a plan that will enable your team to implement the strategy daily.

How to Apply Your Strategy

Strategy comes to life when you and your team can easily apply the choices made in setting your strategy in the daily operations of your company. It's not practical to reference complicated documents or diagrams for every decision, so you need shortcuts for applying your strategy in real time. What you need is a *heuristic*.

Heuristic sounds fancy but is an immensely practical idea. As a field, heuristics are studied by cognitive psychologists, philosophers, attorneys, and even artificial intelligence researchers. For founders, heuristics simply means something like "a rule of thumb." But your branding rules of thumb won't be based on mere guesses or gut-level reactions. Rather, they'll be based on deliberates choices founded in market realties.

"Heuristics" are rules of thumb that will empower your team to apply your strategy in a daily basis.

Once you've built your brand strategy, your team will have plenty of useful heuristics, or rules of thumb, for making decision in real time, without having to consult with you personally or with complicated planning documents.

The ultimate goal, then, is that *your brand strategy should provide you with a shortcut for making strong decisions* that carry out the mandate of your guiding policy. By the time you've finished this book, you'll be able to make brand decisions with confidence, instead of guessing or just "going with your gut."

What kinds of decisions are we talking about? When it comes to brand, you'll face plenty, including: How do you know what colors to use on the web site? What should your homepage headline say? Should your name be funny or serious? Is the tone of your blog playful or corporate? Should your Twitter account tweet the meme du jour or focus on sharing relevant industry news? What types of events should you sponsor?

These are just a handful of the questions you'll face when building a company, and each one has dozens of possible answers. The potential combinations of those choices are practically infinite. Have you ever seen an ad for a burger place that says something like "More than 10 million possibilities"? It seems absurd, but it's just simple math.

To determine the number of possible combinations of a set of items, you calculate the *factorial*. Remember those? It's the number followed by an exclamation point, like 4! That simply means you multiply 4 x 3 x 2 x 1, and that equals 24. Factorials get big fast. If you're making a burger, and the list of ingredients is 10 or 15, all the possible combinations really are in the millions.

And this math is why brand strategy is so important. Every decision you make matters, and the number of choices are near infinite.

And that brings us to *execution*. These decisions all relate to the tangible aspects of a company's brand, including name, logo, URL, web design, tone of voice, and any other element that customers can experience. Executing a strategy is what brings a brand to life, and execution should be based on strategy. See Figure 1-1.

STRATEGY		EXECUTION
Research: • Customer Insight • Competitive Environment	• Positioning • Brand Essence • Values • Personality	• Name • Logo • Design • Language

Figure 1-1. The difference between strategy and execution

The foundation, justification, and point of departure for all external brand artifacts are found within your **brand strategy**. Name, logo, creative direction, URL, web design—these things should all emerge from this common place.

But here's the thing: *most startups skip strategy and go straight to execution.* What's the result of that order of operations? Basically, you have to reinvent the wheel every time they need to go somewhere.

■ Without strategy-based heuristics, startups will reinvent the wheel each time they create marketing and messaging.

Since you have no strategy-based heuristics to rely on, each brand decision is just tacked on to whatever choices were made before. Not only is this approach dilutive to a brand story over time but on a practical level, it means that each time a team makes a decision about these things, they find themselves wasting time discussing every detail over and over again.

Not so with a brand strategy. Once you've developed a brand strategy, decisions about logo design and art direction are all based on a common, well-reasoned foundation.

It's a lot like deciding to build a home. You start with the big picture first, like where to lay the foundation and what style of home you want to build. That way, all your decisions later about finishes and flooring and paint color will be consistent. You'd probably want to avoid something like putting wall-to-wall shag carpet in an industrial concrete loft. But in a sense, startups make a similar mistake all the time.

If brand *strategy* is the structure of a building, the *execution* is the paint and the shutters. Therefore, *designing a logo or building a web site without a brand strategy is much like choosing handles for cabinets in a home that doesn't have a floor plan.*

That's why brand strategy is worth the effort, and that's what this book is all about.

The Impact of Brand Strategy

If you're an early-stage founder, brand strategy may seem like something that can wait till later. You might feel that with so many other priorities, brand should take the backseat to product and engineering considerations. This kind of thinking is a trap.

Without careful consideration and internal alignment, failing to develop a brand strategy will cause countless hours of frustration as you begin to scale your team and your brand. It never seems like a problem *until it's a really big problem*. I've seen it firsthand.

▪ A lack of brand strategy never seems like a problem until it's a really big problem.

I once worked with a C-stage startup that originally launched as a crowdsourcing platform. Crowdsourcing was important for their brand early on, and the word "crowd" was literally in their name. Over time, though, the company pivoted toward data science and machine learning, and the crowd became less relevant.

But while the pivot went well, the company never updated its branding to reflect the new company strategy, and by the time the CEO went to raise a fresh round of funding, the crowdsourcing fad was all but gone.

Unfortunately, this change in environment meant he had to spend the first third of every investor meeting trying to explain why his machine learning company had "crowd" in the name, wasting time and diverting attention from the big picture.

He ultimately closed the round but later said the crowd-centric brand was so distracting it actually hurt their valuation. Needless to say, they rebranded soon after.

This company's business strategy had changed so fast their brand strategy couldn't keep up. As a result, the execution of their strategy—name, logo, web site, etc.—wasn't only irrelevant, it was distracting, and it undermined them in tangible ways.

The Cost of Brand Strategy Debt

This gap between business strategy and brand strategy is common among startups. Without attention, that gap grows, compounds, and becomes harder to correct. It can be tough to spot, though, because the gap widens slowly.

There's a real cost to this gap, but not all are immediately obvious. Here are a few of the more common negatives you can expect if you haven't developed a brand strategy:

Brand Drift

No one seems to be able to describe what you do in any consistent and accurate way—not employees, customers, investors, or the press. Over time, these outdated perceptions of your brand persist in the market, and even though you've updated your brand, you'll have to work hard to reeducate the market and correct those misperceptions.

This course correction down the road means you'll have to spend more time and more money reeducating the market, instead of creating new value for the company and your customers.

Duplicated Effort

As your team creates content, each blog post, tweet, landing page, web page, or marketing will require your team to start from the very beginning, discussing not only the execution but the presumed underlying strategy as well. What kind of GIF would we include? Do we do funny emoji or not? You'll have to rehash these fundamental questions every time.

Unfocused Activities

All those repeated discussions mean your team spends a substantial percentage of their time rehashing decisions that should have already been made.

Diluted Word of Mouth

Your key messages become weakened the further they spread from you, rather than self-perpetuating like a dividing cell. That self-perpetuation is a key benefit to a strong brand, but without a clear strategy, no one will know how to talk about your company.

Reactive Posture

You spend time redefining yourself, often in light of a competitor or peer, rather than leading with high-impact messaging that emphasizes your vision, values, and key differences. You might find yourself saying things like, "We're similar to X, but what's different about is…" or "Yeah, our name is a bit misleading, what we really do is…."

Inefficient Advertising

Solid click-through rates (CTRs) are essential to efficient online advertising, but without a clear message, you risk poor CTRs. As a result, you spend more time and money getting the flywheel spinning, losing out on momentum and leverage while attracting unqualified leads.

Individually, each of those issues might seem insignificant. But in aggregate, what is the total impact on your team's productivity and your company's revenue? It might be tough to measure, but it's real.

Lewis Carroll said, "If you don't know where you are going, any road will get you there." It's also said in advertising circles that if you don't have a strategy, any campaign can take you there. Same thing with branding.

▪ Brand strategy matters for startups because it's what keeps the team aligned and focused on a high-impact story, avoiding brand drift along the way.

The Benefits of Investing in Brand Strategy

What are the benefits of investing early in brand strategy? You can expect several positive outcomes, including the following:

Clarity

All of your marketing materials, like web site, blog, social assets, and campaigns, will deliver the same key message consistently. You'll know what to say and how to say it.

Alignment

Everyone on your team, from full-timers to interns to contractors, will be supplied with those clear messages and equipped to communicate them in their work, whether that's an ad, an email, or UI microcopy.

Efficiency

Since everyone is aligned around clear and powerful messages, you no longer have to spend time thinking about and debating what your communication should look and sound like.

Customer Loyalty

Because you've taken the time to understand your audience, your positioning, personality, and messaging resonate deeply with your customers, endearing them to your brand.

Differentiation

You've assessed the competitive situation and discovered an undeserved opportunity in the market. As a result, you deliver clear messaging to your customers on how you're different.

When to Focus on Building Brand Strategy

It's clear that brand strategy matters, especially for startups. But at what point should it become top priority? Founders have to juggle a ton of concerns—I know, that's an understatement. You're dealing with product, testing, hiring, legal, and financial matters and keeping the board and investors in the loop. And those are just a few large buckets that have to be managed.

I've seen many founders avoid strategic brand thinking for those reasons. But here's the good news: using the tools in this book, several hours invested early will pay off exponentially over time, as you and your team build smart strategy into every decision you make. In this way, implementing your strategy will become second nature.

> Once you've made a handful of key decisions about your strategy, your team can apply the resulting heuristics daily.

That said, there are a handful of inflection points when you might consider a deeper dive into brand strategy, particularly as your brand begins to scale. What does that look like?

In the early days, *you*, the founder, have been the face of the company and the de facto face of the brand as well. *You* go to customer meetings, answer emails, and likely tweet and blog and run support. That's as it should be.

But *as you approach product-market fit, the brand will begin to outgrow you*. That's because you won't have the chance to speak with every customer, and ideally, user adoption is growing far beyond what a single person could drive.

Reporters and bloggers will start writing about you. You may begin experimenting with paid advertising, like AdWords or Facebook Ads. In general, the machine is starting to work.

At this point, brand strategy *really* begins to matter. *Without a strategy, how do you ensure all those different channels are aligned to tell the same, powerful story?* It's no longer something you can micromanage or brute force.

As you scale, there are a few common inflection points that drive the need to invest in brand strategy:

Growth

You've achieved product-market fit, and you've decided to focus on user acquisition. At this point, the team has been heads-down for months, gathering feedback, iterating, building, selling, and just trying to hold it all together.

As a result, no one has taken the time to discuss your brand choices in months, and the last web site refresh happened well before you nailed product-market fit. Your product is good enough that it's growing organically, but your brand is proving a hindrance to faster growth, rather than a catalyst or a force multiplier.

This is a great time to step back and integrate all of your learnings into a cohesive strategy.

Shift in Audience

This scenario is similar to the prior example, but the key difference is that, through your customer discovery, you've learned that that the audience you were originally targeting is no longer your primary market.

This is fairly common in B2B and developer products. For example, your API might have gained traction among a niche developer community early on, but you've learned that the larger markets, and larger budgets, are next door in the marketing department.

In this case, the existing developer-centric brand strategy no longer applies, and probably gets in the way. This is an excellent time to step back, review your strategy, and determine what aspects of your current brand can be preserved and what has to go.

Ongoing Pain

Sometimes, a brand will cause problems regardless of stage. Maybe your team has trouble articulating your value in less than a paragraph, or people says things like, "I love their features, but I'm not really sure what they're all about." Again, it's time to take a look at the strategy.

I'd add one nuance to this discussion: if you haven't achieved product-market fit,[2] I can't in good faith advise you to spend time refining your brand strategy. *Your primary branding goal for now is simply to not look or sound distracting.* Just focus on learning from your customers and building something they love.

But there is one important caveat to this piece of advice: if your name or logo or web site is just awful, even in the very beginning, you probably *are* stacking the deck against yourself, since distracting brand elements might cause trouble with customer discovery or getting useful feedback.

In that case, advisors are likely to spend time suggesting web site edits or ideas for new names, rather than providing feedback on your business model or its underlying assumptions, which is exactly the kind of help you need at this stage.

If that describes you, do your best to course correct for now, and use the tools in this book to start making smart decisions. Focus on the Audience and Competition boxes of the Brand Strategy Canvas, as the research and analysis you conduct for those sections will aide your customer discovery and will be helpful regardless of your final brand strategy.

You might also spend some time on the Values box further down the canvas, since company values exist independent of the specifics of your product or solution. In my experience, it's never too early to begin having values-focused discussions with your cofounders and early team members.

---

[2] Venture capitalist Marc Andreessen summarizes product-market fit as "being in a good market with a product that can satisfy that market." (web.stanford.edu/class/ee204/ProductMarketFit.html)

But at this point, beyond collating your initial research and exploring values, I'd recommend against spending tons of time and money on executing a brand strategy.

That's because until you've reached product-market fit, you're still gathering insights about your customer and your market. And in reality, there are probalby several pivots standing between you and growth mode.

I can't count that times I've seen startups spend time and money on brand execution, then realize they need to pivot, rendering all that work completely irrelevant.

So if you're pre-product–market fit, prepare for the future by reading this book and internalizing the thinking; but primarily, just try not to be terrible for the first little while. That's the long and short of your strategy at this point.

Conclusion

Okay, consider your bases covered! You now have a definition of strategy that you can apply to your brand and to other parts of your business. You've also seen how the kernel of your strategy will translate into heuristics that your team can leverage every day to ensure your messaging resonates with customers and helps you avoid brand drift.

In the next chapter, we'll explore the key aspects of the Brand Strategy Canvas to understand how you can begin crafting a strategy of your own.

CHAPTER 2

Overview of the Brand Strategy Canvas

Starting with a Blank Canvas

Okay, we now understand the difference between strategy and execution and why strategy matters, but *how do you actually **do** strategy*? How do you lay the groundwork so that your team has those powerful heuristics for making smart decisions?

I spent several years in an advertising agency, where I had a front seat to the creative process of some of the best strategic thinking I've ever seen. The creative directors, copywriters, and other strategists combined insights from research with creative intuition to generate ideas that moved minds and industries. Needless to say, it was quite an education.

While there, I learned that creating a powerful strategy involves multiple steps, including different types of research, investigating how all that information fits together, then creatively exploring the most meaningful way to communicate those insights.

© Patrick Woods 2020
P. Woods, *The Brand Strategy Canvas*,
https://doi.org/10.1007/978-1-4842-5159-1_2

Chapter 2 | Overview of the Brand Strategy Canvas

If that sounds ambiguous to you, you're not alone. For many, the strategy development process seems messy and difficult to repeat, and even the top creatives themselves have trouble articulating the specific steps to arriving at a clear strategy.

So how can people without formal training expect to develop and implement effective strategies?

After years of working with amazing creative directors and copywriters, I noticed a theme that would change the way I understood and applied brand strategy:

■ The patterns for discovering a great strategy repeated from client to client, and there was an implicit and repeatable process for developing strategy, time after time.

At the same time, I knew tons of startups wrestling with difficult brand strategy questions. I wanted to help nonexperts build their brands, so we created a tool that would allow anyone to follow the same process the pros use every day. It's called the Brand Strategy Canvas, and we open-sourced it, making it free for anyone to use.[1]

On a single page, the canvas converts the abstract strategy development process into a clear set of steps that you can start using today. The rest of this book will teach you step by step how to use the canvas to build a brand strategy all on your own.

Figure 2-1 shows what a blank canvas looks like.

---

[1] The team at Archer Malmo was instrumental in bringing this vision to life, including Gary Backaus, Dan Price, and Justin Dobbs.

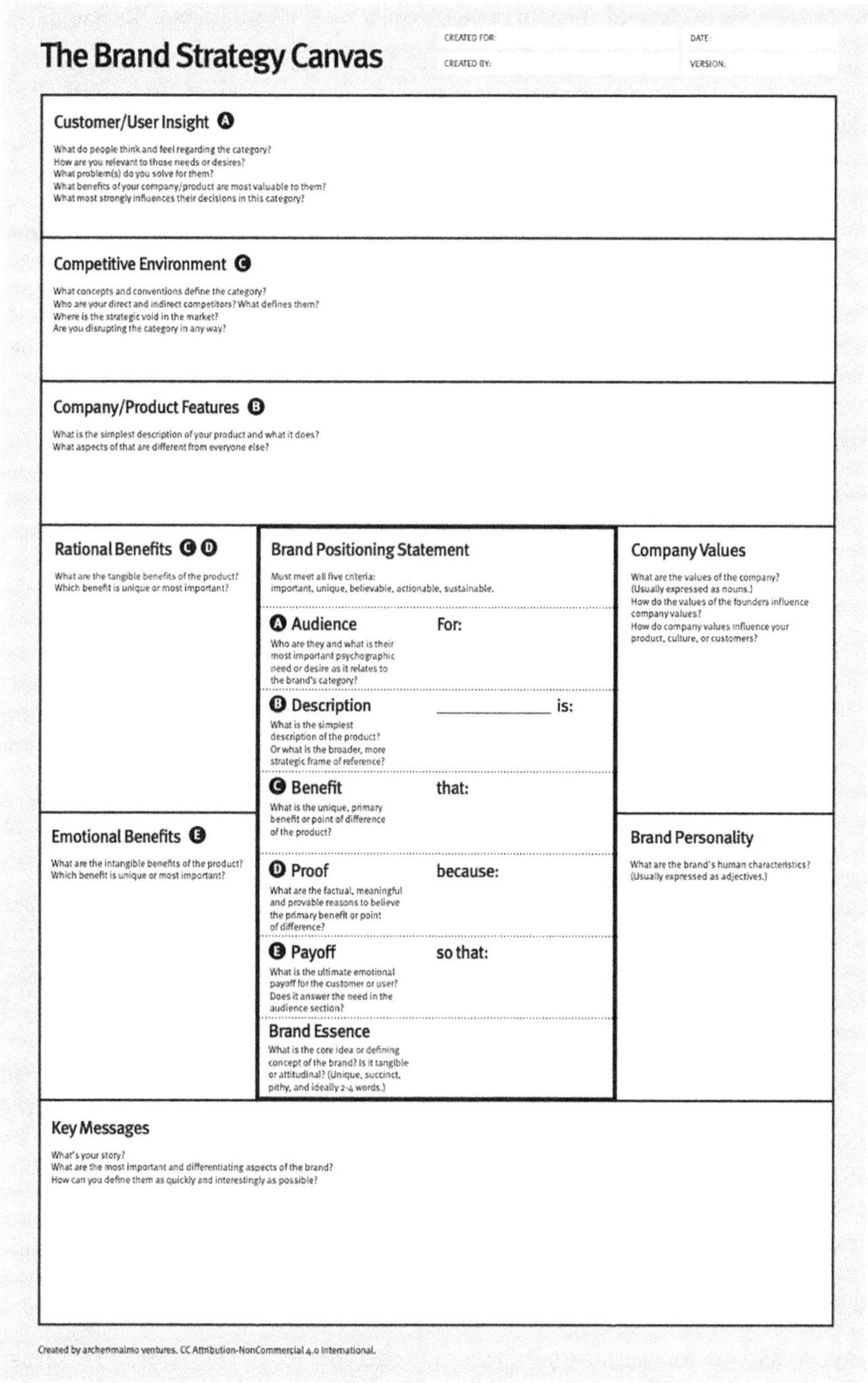

The Brand Strategy Canvas

CREATED FOR: _____ **DATE:** _____
CREATED BY: _____ **VERSION:** _____

Customer/User Insight **A**
What do people think and feel regarding the category?
How are you relevant to those needs or desires?
What problem(s) do you solve for them?
What benefits of your company/product are most valuable to them?
What most strongly influences their decisions in this category?

Competitive Environment **C**
What concepts and conventions define the category?
Who are your direct and indirect competitors? What defines them?
Where is the strategic void in the market?
Are you disrupting the category in any way?

Company/Product Features **B**
What is the simplest description of your product and what it does?
What aspects of that are different from everyone else?

Rational Benefits **C D**
What are the tangible benefits of the product?
Which benefit is unique or most important?

Brand Positioning Statement
Must meet all five criteria: important, unique, believable, actionable, sustainable.

A Audience — For:
Who are they and what is their most important psychographic need or desire as it relates to the brand's category?

B Description — is:
What is the simplest description of the product? Or what is the broader, more strategic frame of reference?

C Benefit — that:
What is the unique, primary benefit or point of difference of the product?

D Proof — because:
What are the factual, meaningful and provable reasons to believe the primary benefit or point of difference?

E Payoff — so that:
What is the ultimate emotional payoff for the customer or user? Does it answer the need in the audience section?

Brand Essence
What is the core idea or defining concept of the brand? Is it tangible or attitudinal? (Unique, succinct, pithy, and ideally 2–4 words.)

Company Values
What are the values of the company? (Usually expressed as nouns.)
How do the values of the founders influence company values?
How do company values influence your product, culture, or customers?

Emotional Benefits **E**
What are the intangible benefits of the product?
Which benefit is unique or most important?

Brand Personality
What are the brand's human characteristics? (Usually expressed as adjectives.)

Key Messages
What's your story?
What are the most important and differentiating aspects of the brand?
How can you define them as quickly and interestingly as possible?

Created by archenmalmo ventures. CC Attribution-NonCommercial 4.0 International.

Figure 2-1. A blank copy of the Brand Strategy Canvas

Chapter 2 | Overview of the Brand Strategy Canvas

Don't let the brevity of the single page fool you. It's simple, but not easy.

The layout of the canvas is based on the intuitive process followed by professional creative teams. During that process, the team explores broad and often divergent concepts of where the brand might go and what it could represent, then edits down the ideas into something powerful and relevant.

As you work through the canvas, you'll do that kind of exploration too, going broad then going deep. And that's great: expansive exploration is an important step during the early phases of strategy development.

But ultimately, the kernel of a strategy comes from making hard decisions about what your brand will and will not become. And that's what the Brand Strategy Canvas is all about: guiding you through a series of choices to discover and refine your brand strategy. It will direct you through a process of **distilling** the essence of your brand.

■ The Brand Strategy Canvas will guide you toward the kernel of your strategy by distilling the essence of your brand.

The idea of "distillation" is key. That's because, in reality, your brand *could* be a lot of things. For example, are you high-end and luxury-focused like early Uber? Or are you more about fun and human connection, like Lyft? Is communicating high quality the most important element of your brand? Or is it more important to demonstrate an approachable personality?

But *of all the things you could be, what should you be*? The distillation of your brand happens through these choices.

As you move through the canvas, you will investigate all the options. Just like professional creatives, you and your team will explore and document all the possibilities and the what-ifs of your brand strategy. The canvas will help you search broadly; then, after that exploration, each section will help you make the hard strategic choices.

Because it's important to understand how all the pieces of the canvas fit together, let's first review each section at a high level before zooming into the deep details of each box. For now, just read through the following overview to get the lay of the land and get familiar with the layout of the canvas and its terminology.

Then, in the following chapters, we'll explore each section in depth and guide you through completing your own canvas, pulling in examples to flesh out the key points of each part of the canvas along the way.

Before moving forward, be sure to download your copy of the Brand Strategy Canvas from www.apress.com/9781484251584, and keep it handy as you work through the rest of the book.

Audience Insight

The first three boxes of the canvas represent your startup's reason for existing: you want to solve a certain problem for a specific group of people who are not being served by the existing options. In these boxes you'll define the gap in the market your company exists to address. See Figure 2-2.

Customer/User Insight Ⓐ

What do people think and feel regarding the category?
How are you relevant to those needs or desires?
What problem(s) do you solve for them?
What benefits of your company/product are most valuable to them?
What most strongly influences their decisions in this category?

Competitive Environment Ⓒ

What concepts and conventions define the category?
Who are your direct and indirect competitors? What defines them?
Where is the strategic void in the market?
Are you disrupting the category in any way?

Company/Product Features Ⓑ

What is the simplest description of your product and what it does?
What aspects of that are different from everyone else?

Figure 2-2. Audience insight

In the **Audience Insight** box, you'll capture key truths about your audience. What are their needs and desires, what are the conceptions of your market?

In the **Competitive Environment** box, you should list key aspects of the competitive situation, including key themes of the category as well as a characterization of key competitors.

Finally, your **Company/Product Features** box will unpack the aspects of your offering that address the needs of your audience and the gaps in the market.

Chapter 2 | *Overview of the Brand Strategy Canvas*

When you overlay truth about your audience, competitive situation, and product features, you should have a clear picture of the strategic opportunity you're going after. It's why you've launched a company in the first place.

These areas represent the springboard into the rest of your brand strategy. Regardless of the decisions you make later about positioning or personality, the market opportunity will stay the same. After all, this section represents the state of affairs from which your opportunity arose.

As a result, when you iterate over your Brand Strategy Canvas, you likely won't see much change in this area.

Benefits

Once you understand how your product features address a need of the audience and exploit an opportunity afforded by the competitive set, you can move on to defining your benefits (Figure 2-3). There are two kinds of benefits: rational and emotional.

- **Rational benefits** speak to how a user *experiences* your brand. It's one step beyond the straightforward description of *what* the thing does and begins moving toward *why* it matters.

- **Emotional benefits** move another step or two up Maslow's hierarchy to arrive at the So what? of the rational benefit.

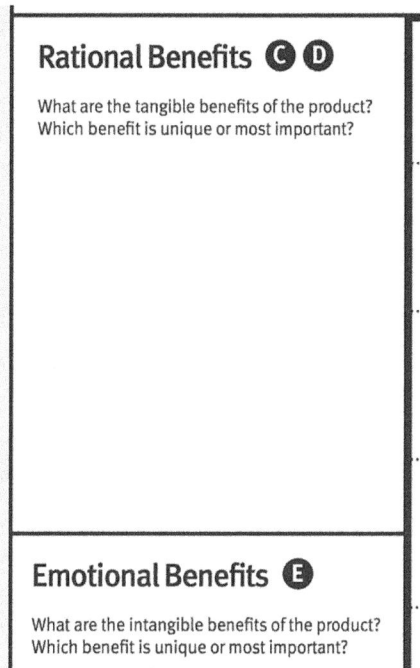

Figure 2-3. The benefits section of the Brand Strategy Canvas

Rational benefits flow out of your product's features, and emotional benefits flow from the rational benefits. As a result, on the canvas, you'll typically move from features to rational to emotional boxes in that order.

Most startup messaging stays at the feature level and never delves into the rational benefits of their offering. Fewer still dig deep enough to uncover the emotional payoffs afforded by the benefits. That's too bad, because, as we'll see later, there's great power in combination of rational and emotional messaging.

Positioning Statement

Once you've completed the boxes in the market opportunity section and have begun listing your benefits, you should have generated enough thinking to begin fleshing out the positioning statement. See Figure 2-4.

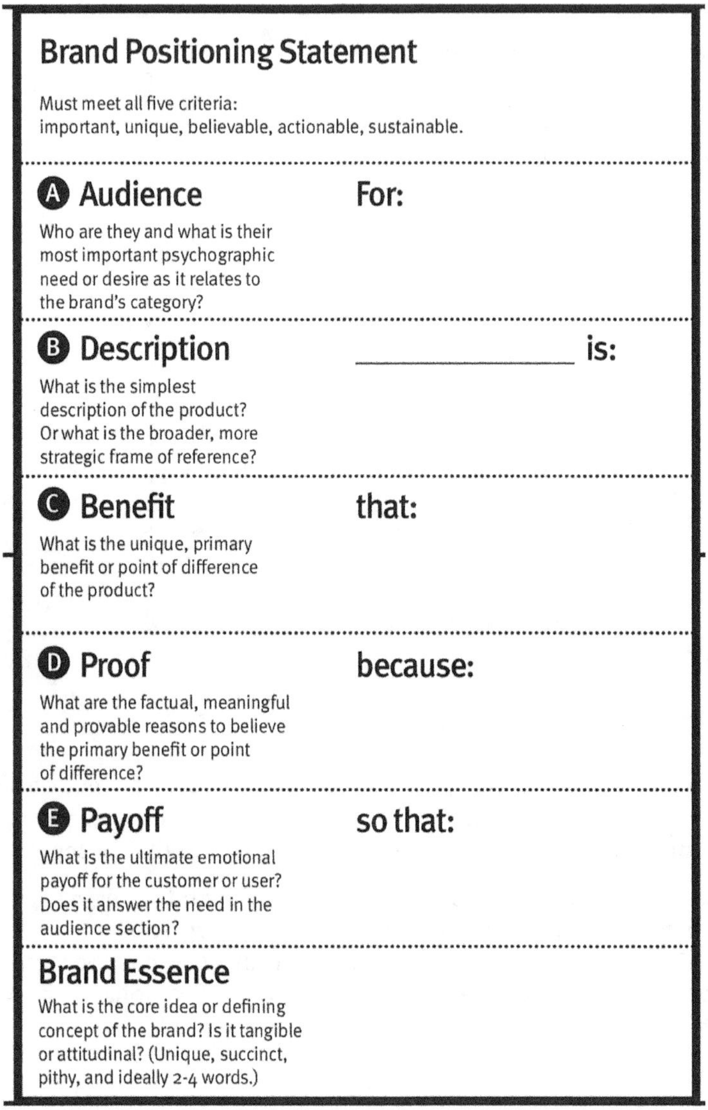

Brand Positioning Statement

Must meet all five criteria:
important, unique, believable, actionable, sustainable.

Ⓐ Audience — For:
Who are they and what is their most important psychographic need or desire as it relates to the brand's category?

Ⓑ Description — _____ is:
What is the simplest description of the product? Or what is the broader, more strategic frame of reference?

Ⓒ Benefit — that:
What is the unique, primary benefit or point of difference of the product?

Ⓓ Proof — because:
What are the factual, meaningful and provable reasons to believe the primary benefit or point of difference?

Ⓔ Payoff — so that:
What is the ultimate emotional payoff for the customer or user? Does it answer the need in the audience section?

Brand Essence
What is the core idea or defining concept of the brand? Is it tangible or attitudinal? (Unique, succinct, pithy, and ideally 2-4 words.)

Figure 2-4. Positioning statement template

The positioning statement is geographically central to the Canvas, and it's philosophically central to your brand strategy as whole.

On the Brand Strategy Canvas, you'll notice many boxes contain a letter next to their names. Those letters correlate to various boxes in the positioning statement. In this way, your positioning statement will pull from the ideas you generated as you worked through each of the preceding sections of the canvas. See Figure 2-5.

The Brand Strategy Canvas

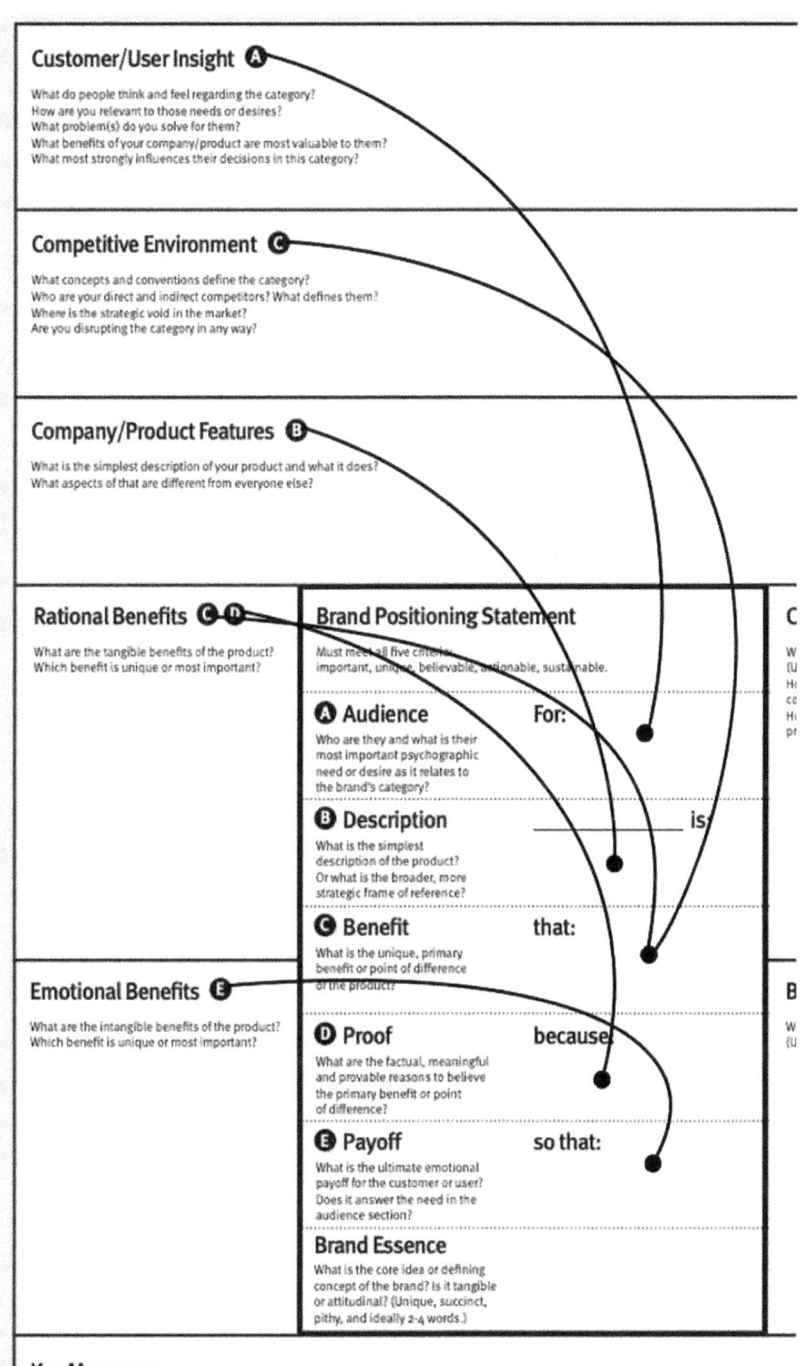

Figure 2-5. How the boxes fit together

For example, you'll see an A in the Customer/User Insight box, as well as in the Audience box of the positioning statement. After you list all the aspects of your customers in the Customer/User Insight box, you'll pick one key idea from that box for the Audience section of the positioning statement. You'll have to choose what's most important.

The final part of the positioning statement is called the brand essence, which distills the primary idea of your positioning statement into a two- to four-word phrase.

Again, the process of brand strategy is fundamentally reductive, and the positioning statement forces you and your team to move from all the things your brand *could* represent toward what specifically your brand *should* represent.

Values and Personality

Unlike the contents of the prior boxes, which can shift based on your business strategy, your values are true no matter what you've learned about the target audience or the competition. Values are internal, typically aren't used in marketing messaging, and from a user's standpoint, they're more experienced than spelled out. See Figure 2-6.

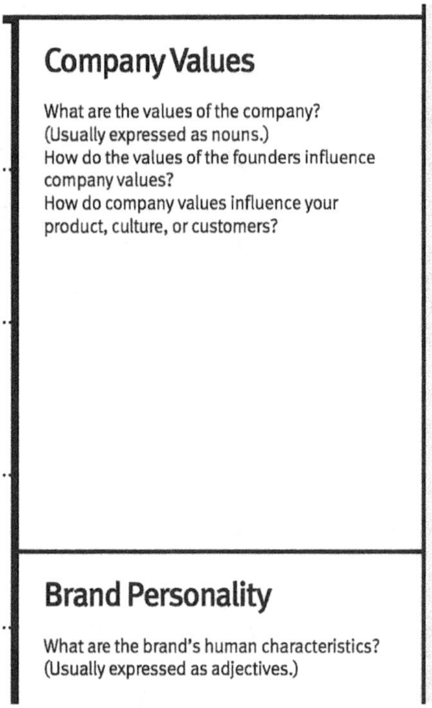

Company Values

What are the values of the company? (Usually expressed as nouns.)
How do the values of the founders influence company values?
How do company values influence your product, culture, or customers?

Brand Personality

What are the brand's human characteristics? (Usually expressed as adjectives.)

Figure 2-6. Company values and personality

They serve a powerful function, however. Once your team has aligned on your values, they will serve as guide rails of your brand choices. In others, your values will help determine what your brand will and will not do and say.

Personality, on the other hand, is the outward manifestation not only of your values but also your positioning. While much of this canvas is totally internal, your personality is where the world begins to interact with who you are and how you view yourself.

Key Messages

Once you understand the market situation and how your positioning statement fits within that context and have spelled out your values and personality, you can develop a handful of talking points that you will communicate across all channels. These aren't necessarily headlines or taglines or usable copy at all for that matter. What we want here is a list of things that are salient and relevant for your audience, based on your positioning, and true to your values. See Figure 2-7.

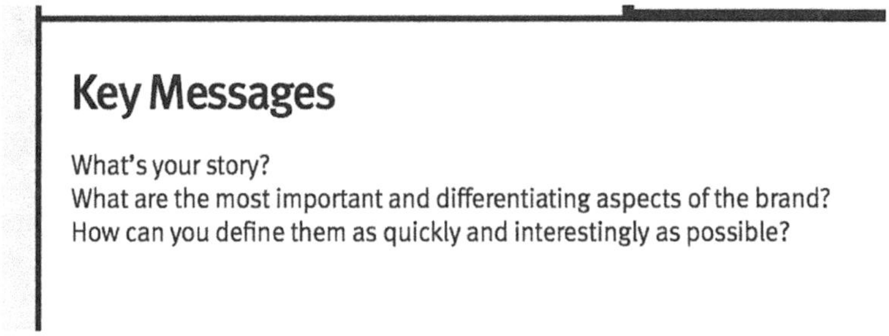

Key Messages

What's your story?
What are the most important and differentiating aspects of the brand?
How can you define them as quickly and interestingly as possible?

Figure 2-7. Key messages

Best Practices and Quick Start Tips

Now that you understand the parts of the Brand Strategy Canvas, let's explore how to maximize the return on your effort as you work through each section. While the canvas certainly provides the framework for powerful work, on its own, it's nothing more than a sheet of paper with some lines. Having a tool is a nice start, but a hammer's no good unless you know how to swing it. Good luck driving home a nail with the claw end.

It's the same with the Brand Strategy Canvas. As with any tool, technique matters. And while this tool is a lot more complex than a hammer, it's also a lot more powerful.

Let's look now at some time-tested methods for getting the most out of the Brand Strategy Canvas.

Start from the Top

The overlapping aspects of the competitive situation, customer insight, and your feature set combine to create the opportunity for your company. If you've done any customer discovery, these first three boxes should be fairly straightforward. As a bonus, using the info gained during customer discovery will help you build momentum as you work your way down the page.

Make Choices

The benefit of a tool like the Brand Strategy Canvas is in reducing the universe of possibilities down to a handful of the most relevant truths about your brand. Start broadly with the first five boxes. Then, when you begin writing your positioning statement, start making choices about which direction you should take. Use a pen along the way. They don't have erasers, and that encourages commitment.

Garbage In, Garbage Out

Like any process, the tool itself is useless without deliberate and thoughtful effort. Done casually, the canvas could be completed in as little as 5 minutes. But it's not a race. If you want results that are true and actionable, you and your team must be willing to ask hard questions, push your assumptions, and move past the obvious.

Work Alone First

Startups are naturally collaborative, so the tendency will be for everyone to work on the canvas together. But here's what I learned from ad agency creative teams: the best work is done when you work as a group to discuss big ideas and frame the problem; then send everyone off to work on their own. After everyone has had time to work through the canvas individually, *only then* should the group come together to compare notes. There are a couple reasons for this.

For one, you'll be surprised how different each team member's canvas will look. It's common that a team will say, "We've got a pretty good handle on our brand. We're all on the same page." But after comparing canvases, it becomes clear that there's a lot divergence in critical areas of the startup's brand strategy. This diagnostic process is one of the most valuable reasons for using a tool like the Brand Strategy Canvas.

Additionally, working alone during the exploratory stage of the creative process is simply good practice. It's the way professional creatives do great work. On *Mad Men*, you might've seen the creative team lounging about, feet up on tables, spitballing ideas. To be certain, that happens. But before working in a group, the best creatives toil away alone, exploring various avenues and approaches.

Finally, group work is often dominated by the strongest personality. If the strongest personality is the CEO's, you can bet other team members won't naturally dive in to contribute to the discussion, especially with differing or opposing viewpoints.

In my experience, it's impossible to achieve deep focus, think intently, and explore the nuance of a particular direction in a group discussion.

Once everyone has spent some time in solo exploration, you'll find that the group discussion is more informed and more fruitful.

Don't Rush It

An important step of the creative process is the simple act of waiting. Walk around any ad agency creative space and you're likely to see art directors brushing up on their ping-pong serves, or overhear writers talking about the recent episodes of *Black Mirror*.

To the untrained eye, this looks like slacking off or good old-fashioned fooling around. But anyone who's worked in the creative fields knows that there comes a point in the creative process where waiting is the absolute best thing you can do to solve the problem at hand.

That's because even though you're focused on taking a walk or taking a few reps at the ping-pong table, your subconscious is hard at work making connections your frontal cortex couldn't imagine. Without fail, there comes a point during this phase of development that many call the Aha! moment, that split second of clarity while you're washing your hair in the shower when somehow the solution just comes to you.

Developing your brand strategy is an inherently creative act and, as such, requires an approach similar to the one advertising creatives follow when developing an ad campaign. You'll be tempted to plow through the Brand Strategy Canvas, to do a couple versions and call it quits.

You'll get the best results, though, when you provide yourself and your team with time to walk away and let your subconscious do the work.

Here's what I suggest: to start, give yourself and the team a few hours to work alone; then reconvene as a group 2 or 3 days later to combine everyone's thinking into a single canvas. Then come together again 3 days later to discuss any refinements, and make your final decisions.

There's no hard-and-fast rule about timing, but in general, you should allow for between 2 weeks and a month from start to finish.

Iterate

One of my favorite Brand Strategy Canvas moments was dropping by a friend's office space in Austin for his startup's launch party. They were in the midst of refining their brand in general, and their name in particular, so I'd shared an early draft of the canvas to aid in the process. He'd mentioned via email that his team found it useful. I thought he was just being his usual kind and thoughtful self.

As I was milling about the party that evening, I came across several copies of the Brand Strategy Canvas printed out, marked up, and pinned to the wall.

His team actually had used the Canvas, and it was clear they'd put in the struggle to refine their thinking. And as it turns out, they continue to look back at the Canvas as a reference point for design and copy choices on an ongoing basis.

The canvas is meant to be printed, reworked, and reprinted. Try different angles in the positioning statement, and explore how the various elements interact. Hang prior versions on the wall to gain an understanding of how your thinking has evolved and become increasingly focused. As you iterate, you'll see how your thinking clarifies and how previously rough and weak positions become increasingly refined.

Consider Multiple Audiences

In many cases, your startup will have multiple audiences, each of whom have different goals and aspirations than the other groups. Marketplaces are great examples of this kind of situation. Consider Upwork, which is a platform for connecting freelance designers and developers with clients who need that kind of work done.

Upwork needs lots of freelancers on their site, as well as a lot of people looking to hire freelancers. As you might imagine, if Upwork were to complete their Brand Strategy Canvas, sections like Customer Insight, Competitive Environment, and Product Features would look very different depending on which group they were talking to.

As a result, *if your company has to message to different audiences, I recommend completing a Canvas for each group*. In the case of Upwork, they would have a canvas for freelancers and a canvas for those hiring freelancers.

That said, multiple canvases are only required when there are major distinctions between various audiences. One way to determine if you need more than one Canvas is to list the desired outcomes for each audience you're considering. For Upwork, one group wants to hire, and the other group wants to *be* hired. For Uber, one audience wants to get a ride, while the other group wants to make money by providing rides.

If, when completing the Customer Insight section of the Canvas, you find yourself wanting to draw a dividing line down the middle of the box to describe each group, you probably need more than one Canvas.

Conclusion

After familiarizing yourself with the structure of the Brand Strategy Canvas, perhaps you can relate to Mark Twain, who once said,

> "I must have a prodigious amount of mind; it takes me as much as a week, sometimes, to make it up!"

As a founder, you certainly have plenty of ideas about your business, your customers, and your product. In the following chapters, we'll walk through each box of the canvas and refine your knowledge and ideas into clear and applicable rules to guide your team and inspire your audience.

CHAPTER 3

Market Opportunity
Laying the Foundations of Your Brand Strategy

Okay, now that you're armed with an understanding of the overall structure of the Canvas, let's dive in to each individual box. The Brand Strategy Canvas begins where you began: with an opportunity in the market. The first three boxes capture that opportunity.

Usually, some insight will be derived from the triangulation of the forces represented by these three boxes that will point the way to a unique brand idea. Let's dive deep into each area, then explore how they fit together.

As you'll see, these three boxes are tightly interconnected, and what you choose to include in one box can and should impact the others. For that reason, you might find yourself working through these first few boxes several times as you explore those relationships.

Customer/User Insight

The first box of the canvas deals with your customers. Since strategy is a heuristic, a shortcut for decision-making, we want to create a clear and compelling picture of your audience so that your team can quickly recall who they're talking to.

Chapter 3 | Market Opportunity

> The goal of this section is to capture the most compelling attributes of your target audience.

Rather than simply listing everything you've ever learned about them, the result will be a memorable portrait of your ideal customer that you can evoke anytime you're creating content.

Instead of writing content for "the customer," or a generic segment, you'll be able to refine and focus your messaging as if you were speaking to a specific person. Just imagine how different it feels when you write an email to a friend vs. when reaching out to a complete stranger.

With the stranger, your tone would probably be a bit formal, and your approach would be general. After all, you don't know this person's personality, if they're funny or serious, or if they would understand the same pop culture references.

Writing to your friend, though, would feel much different. That's because you understand their personality, how they think and feel, and what's on their mind and probably have a sense for their speech patterns and perhaps share a few inside jokes.

Basically, you know how to effectively communicate with the person because you have a rich picture of them in your head based on a deep understanding of who they are.

> The audience part of your strategy will help build a clear picture of your customers so you can always be sure you speaking to the right people in the right way.

Hopefully you have a head start for this section. Since Customer Discovery is a key competency of early-stage founders, it's likely you've spent a lot of time with these folks, which will help as you develop your strategy.

Customer discovery informs product choices, guides decisions about markets to enter, and, in general, provides real-world data for the founding team to test its assumptions against. Customer discovery also proves incredibly useful when outlining your brand strategy, as it will help you create a profile of your audience for you to reference in the future.

To create a memorable profile of your audience, you'll want to consider two types of information: **demographic** and **psychographic** information. While these terms have been around for a while, I've found it helpful to define the two and distinguish between them when describing audiences.

Demographic vs. Psychographic Information

Demographic info consists of all the objective data about an audience, including gender, age, income, location, and a host of other factors. Demographic info answer what, where, and how questions, like what do they do, how old are they, how much do they make, and where do they live?

Here's a fictitious demographic description of a gamer:

> US-based 25–34 year old college-educated males that own one or more gaming consoles and earn more than $40,000 per year.

Yep, that's pretty straightforward.

The other main type of audience description is called **psychographic**, and as the name implies, it explores the psychology of the audience. Unlike demographic data, psychographic starts to dig into the underlying motivations, the why questions. Why do they do what they do? What do their behaviors say about their desires, aspirations, and beliefs? What we're looking for in this case is the "human nature" behind their outward behavior.

As you can imagine, psychographic descriptions are a lot more interesting and inspiring than demographic descriptions alone. The psychological details of your audience help bring to life the facts and figures and will help your team clearly picture who they should be communicating with.

To illustrate, compare the prior demographic description of gamers with this psychographic description.

> Despite having a demanding job and plenty of personal responsibilities, they enjoy unwinding with their friends, often virtually, over casual multiplayer games several times a week; they view gaming as a mature endeavor, and have the income to support this hobby; they believe in working and playing hard.

Which of the two examples paint a more memorable picture of the target audience? The demographic description is straightforward and factual, but the psychographic example begins to paint the picture of the audience. You can probably picture this person in your head and start to feel like you know them a little.

This description doesn't dig into demographic details explicitly, and that's okay. Much of it is implied in things like "demanding job," "personal responsibilities," and "income to support." It's obvious we're talking about adults, so the specifics of the age range wouldn't add much value to the description.

When completing this section of the canvas, most people start with demographic info, since that's what they have handy, but then move toward the more nuanced description as they discuss and explore the facets of their customers.

> Paired together, demographic and psychographic information can provide a clear and powerful picture of your audience.

As you'll see, a well-crafted description illustrates key observations about the customer's psychology and behavior while implying more quantitative demographic data as well.

Uncovering Audience Insights

So how do you discover this kind of info? There are a few methods for researching your audience.

First, get out and talk to people—customers, certainly, but also vendors, partners, employees, and even customers of the competition where possible. In person is great, but video chats and calls are fine. Try to get a sense for who they are, what problems they face, and what they believe.

In addition to product- and problem-centric questions, try to learn about their interests, behaviors, and habits overall. Here are few areas to explore:

- What do they read, both for pleasure and for work?
- What do they do for fun?
- What are their aspirations?
- What personal values are important to them?
- What is their job title and level of seniority?
- How would they describe a typical day at work?

Once you identify the questions that generate the most useful or interesting responses, try to ask the same questions to everyone you interview to identify themes and trends, and be sure to take plenty of notes along the way.

Surveys can be useful if you understand whom you're surveying, especially when they seek to add quantitative metrics to ideas and directions uncovered during your face-to-face discussions.

The Brand Strategy Canvas

You should also consider indirect methods for gathering user insight. Depending on your growth stage, user adoption, and web site traffic, your analytics may contain useful behavioral insights as well. In general, it's important to pore over any information that might provide insight into your user's needs, wants, motivations, and behaviors.

Gleaned from interviews, surveys, implicit behavioral data, or from wherever else, these details should serve as an ever-present guide throughout the creative development process, forming a detailed portrait of your target audience.

From a process standpoint, I would suggest using a tool like Notion to capture as much raw information as possible. I always try to record demographic info in the context of each customer's feedback for slicing and dicing later on.

I'd also suggest capturing as many verbatim quotes as possible. Many of my most powerful brand insights have come directly from customer interviews, so avoid the temptation to simply summarize as someone talks.

But research and information gathering are just the first parts of this step. As discussed, the primary goal of this section of the canvas is to paint a clear picture of your audience by selecting their most compelling wants and needs, as discovered during research. Our goal is to transform our collection of notes and observations into a memorable portrait of our target audience.

Now let's dig into an example.

WALKING THROUGH AN EXAMPLE

Throughout this book we'll use a fictitious strategy for Mailchimp to explore how each box of the canvas comes to life, with a few other example companies sprinkled in along the way. Mailchimp hasn't asked me to develop their brand strategy (yet!), so the assumptions we make here are purely theoretical and for the sake of discussion.

So why Mailchimp? First, the Mailchimp brand is well-developed and widely known, so you'll be able to see how choices made and the strategic level can be experienced by consumers in the execution of the brand.

Also, Mailchimp competes in a competitive and fragmented market, so comparing the competition's brands will give us a fuller picture of how positioning and messaging impact a brand's ability to compete.

Okay, so how might Mailchimp describe its target audience? For each box of the canvas, we'll look at the example entry, then discuss its implications.

Example Audience Description

Small business owners or heads of marketing; understand the power of platforms, but are not overtly technical themselves; recognize the power of integrations; appreciate solid design but also rely on data for decision making; expect powerful features delivered in an elegant interface; want a partner they can grow with; feel like they have good taste

In this example, we've characterized a business owner or a marketer who has high expectations, blending an appreciation for great design with a need to base decisions on data. They're not software developers, but thanks to services like Zapier and IFTTT, they're comfortable integrating various platforms for maximum impact.

At the same time, they want to avoid having to learn countless platforms for managing various parts of their marketing stack. Their ideal partner would provide the right tools at the right time, then grow with them over the long haul.

This kind of customer is less concerned with low price points and is more interested in a great experience. After all, they spend a good deal of time working inside their marketing tools and have come to expect those tools to deliver best-in-class user experiences. Many of them are small business owners, so price is a consideration, just not the decision driver.

At this point, *you might notice that the description is totally psychographic*. There's no mention of income or age or gender. In this case, those factors don't matter. This description could cover males, females, young, or old.

It definitely *implies* something about income, that is, user experience is more important than price. But it's not so much about the company size or revenue. We're talking to people who value their time and are willing to pay a premium for a painless experience.

Additionally, the Mailchimp user *has taste*. They perceive themselves as making deliberate choices about their personal style, the design of their office, the music they listen, the tools they use, and more.

To understand the impact of the choices for each part of the strategy, we'll also explore counter examples to see illustrates how small decisions can have a big impact on your stray.

For example, *imagine all the other ways a marketing platform could describe their target audience*. They could focus on mid-market private companies, global enterprises, or the Fortune 100. They might qualify their audience as companies that have dedicated email marketing team members within a larger marketing department.

You can also imagine a competitor's audience description focusing on skill level, perhaps tailoring a brand to people who are interested in email marketing but who have no clue where to start.

Another common audience feature is price sensitivity. For discount brands, price is a huge factor for their customers, and you can bet a budget band would mention budgets or prices in the audience description, maybe along the lines of "they operate within tight margins, so budge is always a consideration," or "their department is usually a cost-center, so they often give priority to low-cost solutions."

As you consider your audience, what are the behavioral traits your customers share? What common threads have emerged from your conversations with them? Maybe they all really hate something about their current solution. Perhaps saving time is more important than saving money in the near term. Maybe they all listen to obscure indie bands and spend their free time perfecting the nuance of coffee roasting.

In the example, there are lots of things we *could* say about the customer, but these are the insights that rise to the top.

As you'll see, there's a nearly unlimited inventory of descriptors for each section. **But the brand strategy process is all about choosing what's most meaningful for you brand based on what you know about the customer, the market, and your product.**

Whatever the case, this section is all about crafting a description of your audience that is both true, meaningful, and actionable. As we'll see later, how you describe your users will have lasting impact on our brand strategy.

THOUGHT STARTERS

For each section of the canvas, I'll provide a few questions to kickstart your exploration. You don't have to answer each one verbatim, and they shouldn't limit your discussions. Just view them as a way to get started.

- What behaviors or activities are common across your customer base?
- What do they believe about the world?
- What do they believe about themselves?
- What problems do you solve for them?
- What do they read, both for pleasure and for work?
- What do they do for fun?

- What are their aspirations?
- What personal values are important to them?
- What is their job title and level of seniority?
- How would the describe a typical day at work?
- Are they more interested in price or quality?
- How would you describe your customer in one sentence?

Competitive Environment

You now have a clear and memorable picture of your audience, their motivations, and their needs. If the previous section was all about who your customers are, this section is about where they live: the market. In this part of the canvas, we'll look at how the market is, or is not, meeting their needs.

This section is less about listing out your competitors. You've probably already done that, and you may even have them all on a slide in your investor deck. Knowing the competition *is* important, to be sure, but when crafting a strategy, you must go beyond simply knowing their names.

Knowing Your Category

The real power of this section of the canvas is about understanding and describing the key concepts of the *category*. A "category," sometimes referred to as industry, is a way to conceptually group related companies. Sometimes, a category is a subset of an industry.

For example, the industry might be consumer packaged goods (CPG), and the category might be toothpaste. Some categories are well-defined, like those within CPG, but for startups, sometimes the category isn't so clear.

> A good shorthand for "category" is simply the group of competitors who provide a solution to the problem your product addresses.

Why is it important to understand your category? Because understanding the category means understanding your customers' expectations. And now that we understand our customer, that's exactly what we need to do next.

We want to uncover ways in which other companies address their needs, what trends are common among the competition, and the overall features and benefits that seem important to defining the category.

Once you understand your customer's challenges and needs, and what they expect from the category, you'll begin to understand *what's at stake* for your audience.

The goal of this section is to distill all the information about your category into a memorable description that summarizes the competitive situation from the customer's point of view and specifies what's at stake for them.

That way, when you move on to execution later, you'll know how to communicate the ways your offering is distinctive.

So what are the steps for assessing your category? Remember, a key aspect of this exercise is describing the situation from the customer point of view, not your own. To move from an internal view to an external one, you should focus on unpacking the *functional* and *emotional* aspects of both your *direct* and *indirect* competition.

Functional and Emotional Aspects of Your Category

Functional aspects include nuts-and-bolts data points like feature and pricing matrices. These are the objective and inarguable aspects of your competition. Maybe everyone in your category offers a free trial as well as an annual plan. Perhaps they all offer a specific type of partner integration. The features are gated and price is also an important data point to note. You'll definitely want to keep track of all these functional aspects.

But a powerful assessment will go beyond that and look to the **emotional** aspects of the competitive brands. That includes their language and vocabulary, their design choices, and the overall tone and personality of the category. Do they use bright colors or muted tones? Do they use photographs of people, or have they adopted an illustration-based approach? Does their copy feel aspirational or inspirational, or is it very direct and to the point?

Taken together, the functional and emotional aspects of your category will start to give you a sense for the approach of each individual competitor but also the overall themes and trends of the market where you compete.

With that in mind, let's unpack the differences between direct and indirect competition.

Direct and Indirect Competitors

As you assess the market, there are two types of competitors you should consider: direct competitors and indirect competitors. A **direct competitor** is what usually comes to mind when thinking about the competition. They offer the same things you offer, and on the surface, there's a clear choice between your product and their product. Think Coke vs. Pepsi—pretty straightforward.

On the other hand, **indirect competitors** can be harder to identify but are incredibly important to understanding the shape of your market, especially when introducing a new product or solution. You can think of indirect competition in two ways.

First, *how was your audience solving their problem before you came along?* I call this kind of indirect competition *existing alternatives*. For example, if your potential customers were using spreadsheets to solve their problem, then that spreadsheet is your indirect competitor, and your brand will have to overcome the entrenched habits as a result.

In your category, what existing alternatives are your customers currently using? What do they like about those solutions, and what frustrates them?

Second, *you should consider what budget your tool will compete for.* This type of indirect competition is called budgetary incumbents. Let's say you're selling your product into HR teams. In addition to the direct competitors and various existing alternatives, you'll also want to keep in mind how that type of customer buys and how they think about budget allocation.

For example, will you have more success with HR teams that are more focused on compliance or those that are interested in learning and development? In each scenario, how will your buyer be able to get new budget for your solution, or would signing with you mean another person or another team loses budget? What are the budgetary incumbents you'll need to deal with?

There are accepted practices and norms for many fields, and understanding those kinds of preexisting processes will help you understand the reality of your market.

Most "The Competition" slides I've seen in early pitch decks focus entirely on the direct competition and highlight purely functional differences among them. As a result, they don't provide a clear picture of the competition and the overall market.

So how does understanding the direct/indirect distinction help build a brand? Interestingly, it helps when there are too many competitors but also when it seems as if there are no competitors at all.

The Brand Strategy Canvas

First, consider a category with lots of direct competition. Email service providers are a great example—there are countless offerings with little discernible difference. If you were a small business owner deciding to roll-out an email newsletter, how would you choose?

Since you listen to a lot of small business-focused podcasts, you've heard a million ads for Mailchimp. But at an industry event a couple months back, you heard a talk from a woman from Constant Contact. It seems legit as well. But what about VerticalResponse, iContact, and GetResponse?

To be sure, each company offers a toolset that is in some way unique. But only the savviest users will take time to research the options and fully appreciate the nuances between each.

In categories with many similar competitors, brand is often the primary differentiator for top-of-the-funnel customers.

It's the quickest and easiest way for an overwhelmed customer to start conceptually grouping potential vendors. Just compare the home pages of Mailchimp and Constant Contact for a quick look at how different brand executions frame up the conversation.

If you find yourself in a situation where there's plenty of parity across the competition, it's important to be aware of the differences in personalities and messaging across the category. Are all the competitors buttoned-up B2B-style companies? Or is the space generally friendly and approachable? When features are largely the same, a compelling brand might be your best bet for differentiation. But the only way to get there is by first understanding the competition.

In other cases, an early-stage founder might reasonably say, "We have no competition, as we've created the first solution of this kind." It may be true that your widget is the first of its kind, but you only have a business insofar as there is a market willing and able to buy that widget.

And if potential customers exist, they're almost certainly using something else to solve the problem currently. *At the very minimum, you're competing for budget or attention.* Remember the different kinds of indirect competition? How will the existing alternative and budgetary incumbents influence how you positioning yourself to your audience?

Netflix CEO Reed Hastings captured this idea when he said,

> "You get a show or a movie you're really dying to watch, and you end up staying up late at night, so we actually compete with sleep."[1]

Interestingly, he didn't characterize the competition as Redbox or Amazon Prime but rather the indirect alternatives to his service.

In your case, what is the shape of your market? Maybe it's filled with head-to-head direct competitors. Or perhaps, you'll have to dig a little deeper, or look more broadly, at user behavior to understand the alternatives and how you fit in.

Ultimately, in light of the customer insight captured in the prior box, what are the key elements of the competitive set, and where does your solution fit into that mix?

Example Competitive Environment

> Feature parity has led to fragmented offerings, with some focusing on small business, others on e-commerce, and still others focusing solely on email marketing; generally overwhelming messaging; confusion about what benefits actually matter; endless pricing models

For Mailchimp, the competitive environment consists of a fragmented landscape, complicated by the fact that it has evolved beyond a simple email service provider (ESP) to a more full-service online marketing platform, covering multiple channels beyond email. As a result, it faces competition from a few different types of competitors.

Some of the competitors focus almost entirely on email marketing. Constant Contact and AWeber are examples here. They say things like "Powerful email marketing made easy" and "The email marketing platform built for you." Strong feature parity characterizes these competitors, as does a lack of brand personality.

Other competitors, like Drip, focus their messaging on specific niches, like e-commerce. In fact, drip goes so far as to describe itself as an ECRM: an e-commerce CRM.

Others still position themselves as all-in-one solutions for online marketing, like GetResponse, which offers email, marketing automation, landing pages, webinars, e-commerce, surveys, and even a CRM.

---

[1] www.newsweek.com/netflix-binge-watch-sleep-deprivation-703029

As you can see, there are lots of players offering nearly endless features. To top it off, most of the competition delivers its messaging in a straightforward and direct tone, with headlines like "Create professional email campaigns" and "All-in-one online marketing solution to help you grow your business."

Looking back at our example market description for Mailchimp, we haven't focused on individual competitors. Of course, that process can be important from a business model standpoint, and I'm fairly certain you have a slide in your pitch deck that includes a chart with competitors listed vertically and features listed horizontally.

But remember, the goal of this section is to *characterize the landscape with an emphasis on how your customer makes a decision.*

Listing features, in a sense, is company-centric, in that you are comparing yourself to other companies from your own perspective. That's different from walking in the customer's shoes and analyzing the category based on their wants, needs, and perceptions.

THOUGHT STARTERS

- What does your customer experience when researching solutions to their problem?
- What are the words, phrases, and challenges they search for?
- What do they find confusing or overwhelming?
- What are the table stakes, that is, what aspects are standard across all companies in the category?
- What concepts and conventions define the category?
- Who are your *direct* competitors?
- Who are your *indirect* competitors?
- What most strongly influences your audience's decisions in this category?
- What functional benefits are common across the competitions?
- What emotional benefits seem to stand out?
- Where is the strategic void in the market? What are the competitors missing?
- Are you disrupting the category in any way?

Company/Product Features

By this point, you have a clear picture of who your customers: what they like and don't like, challenges they deal with, and their expectations, hopes, and habits.

You've also created a rich landscape of the market where these customers live, which provides you with a rich picture of their experience in solving their main challenge. That includes common issues they face, the typical offerings from peers and competitors, and a robust landscape of what's in the market.

The logical question now is, where can they turn for help?

With the full context of the first two boxes, in the third and final box of the market opportunity section, you'll answer that question by describing the specifics what you offer. It's your response to the market opportunity.

You may have lots of features, so this section is less about simply listing everything you do. Rather, what you write here should be based on what you know about your users and the opportunity afforded by the competitive environment.

What you list here may feel obvious to you: You and your team know all about your features, why bother writing them down? But this isn't simply an exercise in making a list of known quantities. There are two ways a clear articulation of your most important features will help you build your brand strategy.

Finding Your Reasons to Believe

The first is what we call **reasons to believe**, and they're foundational to a believable brand strategy. Reasons to believe are the tangible proof points for the claims you make about your brand.

For example, just imagine if an apparel brand claimed that they were passionate about protecting the environment through sustainable manufacturing and ran a lengthy campaign bragging about their ideals. Then imagine that a week later you read an article revealing that all their factories are proven to contribute to pollution in developing countries.

How would you feel about that brand? I'd guess indifferent at best and straight up hostile at worst, and you certainly wouldn't believe any of their messaging in the future. Dishonesty is dangerous for people as well as brands.

As we'll see later, the claims you make about your brand must be grounded in truth. The foundation for that truth starts here, with unpacking the tangible features of your offering.

Points of Differentiation

The second reason the features box of the canvas deserves attention is because features are one way you **differentiate** from the competition. My guess is that you have a unique perspective on your audience and market and have built a product to satisfy that opportunity.

In this box, include all those things that make you unique, with specific emphasis on the elements of your product that most powerfully address the market opportunity. In other words, for this type of person with this type of problem, *these* are the things that really matter.

Since you're aiming for differentiation, you should try to avoid the table stakes of your category. Table stakes are the things that you and all of your competitors offer, which should be obvious after your competitive deep dive in the prior section.

It's best to leave out the table stakes, since, by definition, they're no different from your competition and won't impact your customer's decisions to choose you over someone else.

With reasons to believe and differentiation in mind, here's the goal of this section: to capture the most differentiating aspects of your offering, based on what your customers desire and how your competition is servicing those needs.

That goal may sound lofty, but for now, the description should be straightforward. It's not about using creative language or copy just yet. At this point, you're trying to capture core truths about your product. Keep it simple and true.

Example Company/Product Features

> *Comprehensive integrated platform; beautiful experience design; thorough guides and resources; 24/7 help; experts directory; culture of caring; email designer, automation, segmentation, split testing, reporting, landing pages, postcards, forms, Google, Facebook, and Instagram, ads, integrations*

In the Mailchimp example, you begin to see how the Audience Insight and Competitive Environment affect the description of features. We know our ideal users want a partner that can handle their needs at various stages of growth and don't want to spend time learning endless platforms. They just want something that works.

For the DIY members of the audience, Mailchimp provides helpful and engaging training materials for all skill levels, allowing lower-paying customers to self-serve their own education.

For those that want a helping hand, they curate a list of approved partners. On top of all that, they provide round-the-clock support.

All of this is delivered with a beautiful interface by a company with a strong culture of caring.

You can see how these claims are all objectively true. They're also edited for precision in addressing the market opportunity. In other words, Mailchimp *could* list more than a hundred features here. But they've chosen the most differentiated reasons to believe.

What about the competition? While offering many similar features, they fail to communicate those features in a way that resonates with their audience, leaving them confused and overwhelmed.

As we'll see, Mailchimp not only provides tangible features that address the needs of the customer, but they communicate that power in a way that's clear and energizing for the target audience.

Notice how the description moves beyond simple bullet points toward ideas like an *intuitive* user experience and a *culture* of caring. You can do this for your company too, as long as they're true.

This approach marks a shift from straightforward features like 2.5-liter v8 engine, anti-lock brakes, and 24-inch tires, toward less-tangible elements as points of differentiation, like emotion and culture. And as we'll see later, culture can serve as a powerful differentiator.

> **THOUGHT STARTERS**
>
> - What is the simplest description of your product and what it does?
> - What aspects of that are different from everyone else?
> - What are the intangible features that stand out?

Linking the First Three Boxes

Now that we've completed the first three boxes, notice the relationship between your customers, competition, and product, and assess how much the contents of each box relates to the choices you made in the others.

You should note several relationships between the three boxes and the overlap of the concepts in each. See Figure 3-1.

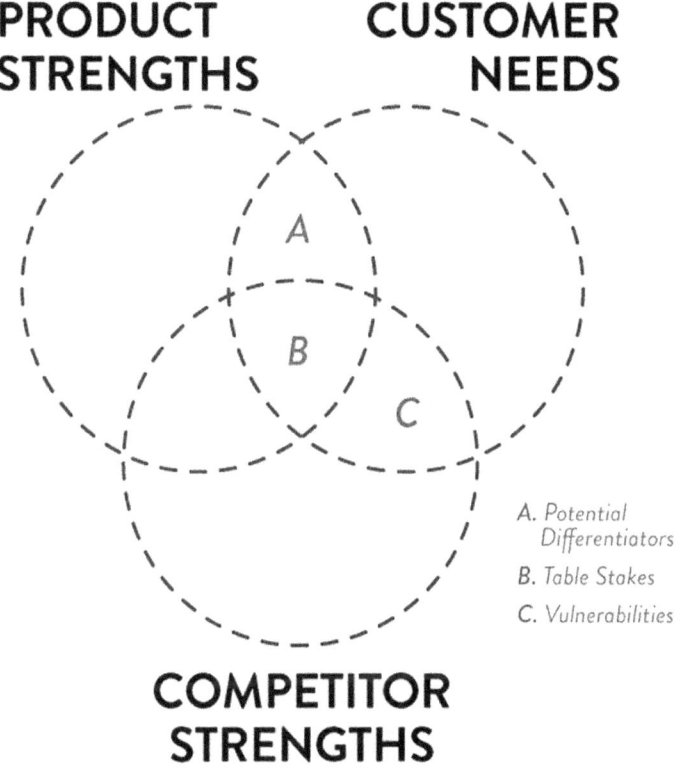

Figure 3-1. The relationship between Product, Audience, and Competition[2]

First, notice area A, which is where your product meets the needs of your audience in ways that are distinct from competitors' strengths. These areas might serve as clear points of differentiation when you develop messaging later in the canvas.

The overlap of all three circles, area B, represents the table stakes mentioned earlier in the chapter. Your customers are interested in these features, sure, but everyone, including you *and* your competition, offers them, so those features probably don't need to be called out on your canvas.

---

[2] This diagram is inspired by Joel E. Urbany and James H. Davis, "Strategic Insight in Three Circles." *Harvard Business Review*, November 2007, hbr.org/2007/11/strategic-insight-in-three-circles.

Finally, area C speaks to those features that your customers and only your competitors provide. If you find a lot of overlap there, your brand strategy may not help you compete, and you might consider other more product-focused soul searching as a result.

As you review the contents of your Brand Strategy Canvas, is there a logical relationship? Or does this section read like three independent and unrelated lists?

If that's the case, that's totally okay. You can simply print more versions of the canvas and iterate. Working through the canvas multiple times will help refine you're thinking, which will lead to a stronger strategy.

That's because *the things you include in these boxes will inform the backbone of your strategy: the positioning statement.* Here's how seemingly subtle choices early in the process can have a big impact later on.

Imagine if, in the Customer Insight box of our example, we described a different segment of the audience, like those looking for simple and cheap email newsletter management. How would that impact the features we highlight?

In that case, things like an "integrated platform" and "24/7 support" sound pretty expensive. And a "culture of caring" sounds pretty fluffy to someone looking for the least expensive possible option. As a result, a different mix of features might make more sense.

Or, what if in Competitive Environment we limited the description strictly to email service providers? How would that impact the way we describe the audience? Instead of including "marketing leaders," we might get more specific and mention "heads of email marketing" or "email marketing specialists."

You can imagine how slightly different choices in one box of leads to other changes across the canvas.

And that's really the case with all boxes of the Brand Strategy Canvas. What you record in one box can greatly affect what ends up in other boxes.

That's because brand strategy is built upon a series of interconnected choices about who you are and how your brand will interact with the world.

Without following a process such as this, you can see how difficult it would be to keep up with each choice about your brand and to see the relationship across each facet of your strategy.

Conclusion

With the Market Opportunity section complete, you've laid the foundation for deeper exploration of your brand strategy and have taken the first steps toward ensuring that your brand heuristics always point to truth about your audience and market.

The first three boxes are true no matter what choices you make later about personality, voice, and key messages. Later, we'll begin transition from the factual truths about your product to the more expressive and emotional ways to talk about your offering with your audience. This shift from what to say to how to say it best begins to occur in the next section, where we'll explore the relationship between features and benefits.

CHAPTER 4

Rational and Emotional Benefits

A Process for Discovering Your Brand Differentiation

So I have a confession: I spend *a lot* of time checking out the web sites of startups. Sometimes they're clients, other times they're friends, and sometimes they're just interesting companies I want to learn more about. I'm a bit of a startup web site junky.

On most any startup web site, in addition to big headlines and large and friendly illustrations, you'll almost always find a link in the navigation called Features. See Figure 4-1.

Click that link, and you'll inevitably land on a page with lots of screenshots and even more bullet points. Prepare yourself for lots of adjectives, too—delightful, clean, beautiful, curated.

© Patrick Woods 2020
P. Woods, *The Brand Strategy Canvas*,
https://doi.org/10.1007/978-1-4842-5159-1_4

The amount of unfounded superlative claims threatens the credibly of the company and the sanity of the reader. This kind of language is often accompanied by lists of phrases describing the product.

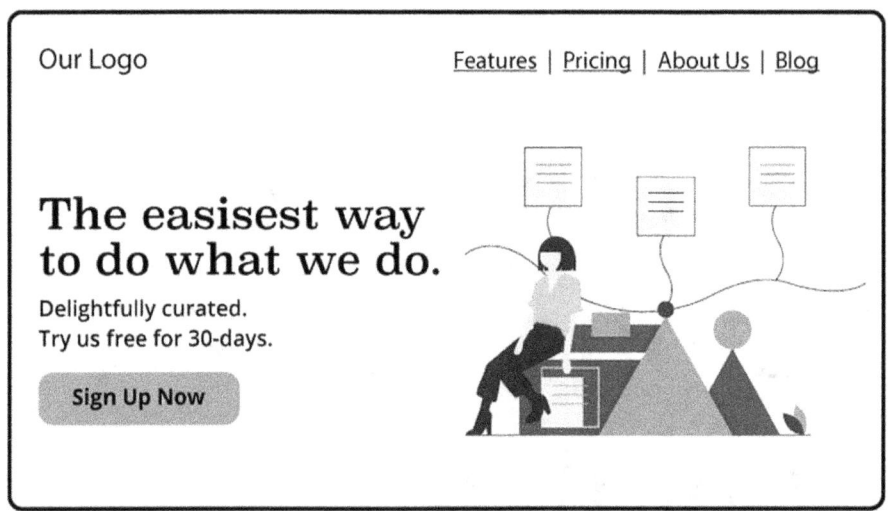

Figure 4-1. Example of a generic web site homepage

Most of the time, the Features page is all about showing the user *what the product does*. At first, that seems pretty logical. It's obviously important to help users understand what you offer, so on one level, a page like this *is* helpful. But telling visitors what your product does and how it works is just the starting point, not the finish line.

What if your Features page could do more than simply describe what happens when your users sign in and start clicking things? What if you could use that space to connect with the reader on a deeper level?

Of course, the Features page on your site is just one tangible expression of your brand strategy, and it happens to be a highly visible illustration of the fact that startups too often focus on features instead of benefits. But far beyond web site copy, we'll see how understanding and articulating your features will become central to a powerful brand story.

Speaking of stories, how much do you think you'd enjoy someone "telling you a story" by simply giving you a list of the key plot points? Something like, "There was a Hobbit who lived happily in a hole, until one day he came across a magical ring. He and his friends had second breakfast while escaping the bad guys."

This straightforward list does in fact communicate events that happened, but would you call it a story? A list of key points like that can be useful to communicate a synopsis of a story, sure, but no one would stick with a 500-page novel or a 3-hour film that simply rattled off the laundry list.

No, the stories that stick with us are the ones that move us, that bring us into that action, and that evoke a meaningful transformation. The same goes for brands.

A powerful brand moves beyond *factual claims* into the realm of *story and emotion*.

And the science proves it. Advertising professionals have always suspected that emotion impacts how people consider and remember brands, and psychology and neuroscience continue to verify that suspicion.

fMRI shows that when evaluating brands, people rely mostly on *emotions* over objective information, like features and facts, and that positive emotions toward a brand have greater influence over brand loyalty than factual brand attributes.[1] As Dr. Jill Bolte Taylor claims in her TEDx Talk,

> "Humans aren't thinking creatures who feel, but feeling creatures who think."

In addition to enabling powerful storytelling, there's also the practical reasons for moving beyond a feature focus, which we discussed in the last section: the fact that features themselves are largely indefensible. Outside of patent protection, competitors can simply copy your features. If you're successful, they almost certainly will.

Before you know it, everyone in your space will offer the exact Features page on their site, and your audience will become increasingly indifferent to which solution they use. Everyone's the same, so why bother understanding the nuance of each product? Just give me the cheapest one.

In a category defined by *feature parity* (that's the technical term for when companies all offer the same things), one way to build a lasting competitive advantage is through your brand, because there's more to a brand than the underlying features.

Competitors can't copy the emotional resonance you create through your brand. So how do you do that?

---

[1] www.psychologytoday.com/us/blog/inside-the-consumer-mind/201302/how-emotions-influence-what-we-buy

Chapter 4 | Rational and Emotional Benefits

> The path to building emotion into your brand begins with an understanding of the relationship between features and benefits.

The two are related, but not the same. And while the distinction might seem apparent to anyone who's ever taken any business course, very few founders appreciate the difference, and fewer still communicate on benefits over and beyond features.

In this chapter, we will unpack the relationship between features and benefits and apply a framework that will help you clarify two kinds of benefits that will impact your brand strategy. Before diving into the specifics of each type of benefit, let's take a moment to lay the groundwork with some key concepts.

The Features-Benefits Continuum

If you've ever studied marketing, you likely have seen a chart with Features listed at the top of the left column and Benefits posted at the top of the right (Figure 4-1). The point of such a chart is to demonstrate the relationship between a feature and its benefit.

If we were talking about a new SUV, on the left, you might see "Roof Rack," and on the right, "Carry more gear." One feature = one benefit. See Figure 4-2. This approach is a straightforward way to communicate to business school students that every feature should have a clear benefit that customers can understand.

STANDARD FEATURES/BENEFITS CHART

FEATURES	BENEFITS
Roof rack	Carry more gear
4-wheel drive	Drive in all conditions
Keyless ignition	Comfy when you get in
V8 engine	Tow heavy loads

Figure 4-2. Example chart of features and benefits

The Brand Strategy Canvas

But while I think the simple features-benefits chart is a useful starting point, it stops short of enabling the kind of emotional storytelling great brands strive for.

To uncover that kind of emotion, I like to take the existing approach one step further and think of two levels of benefits: **rational and emotional**.

Here's how each piece fits together:

- A *feature* is something a thing does.
- The *rational benefit* is how the user experiences that thing.
- The *emotional benefit* is the higher-order payoff of that experience. It's the So What? that originates in the feature itself.

As we'll see, one feature might have multiple rational benefits, each of which might have multiple emotional benefits as a result. See Figure 4-3.

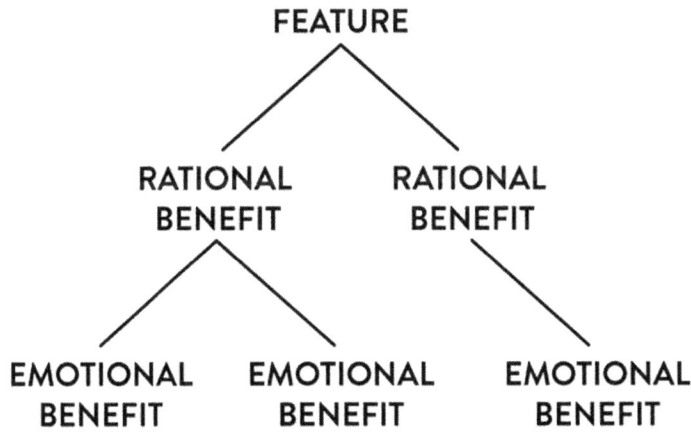

Figure 4-3. The relationship between a feature, its rational benefits, and its emotional benefits

Let us consider another example. If you've ever been on the Apple web site or visited an Apple Store, you'll see that for its MacBook Pro line, Apple offer offers dozens of features across its various models.

One of the most practical, and probably my favorite, is the solid-state hard drive, or the SSD. The retina screen truly is impressive, the Touch Bar is actually kind of neat, and the lightweight and slim profile are killer too. But it's the SSD that I value daily.

Chapter 4 | *Rational and Emotional Benefits*

The SSD is a **feature**. It is an indisputable thing that is true about the MBP. You can imagine Apple listing the SSD in the Features box on their brand strategy canvas, and they definitely list it on their web site.

One **rational** benefit is that the computer boots faster than traditional mechanical hard drives. In other words, I experience the SSD through faster boot times and faster application loading.

So what's the emotional payoff? You can imagine that there might be multiple options, and we'll explore different approaches below. But for the sake of discussion, one **emotional** payoff of the faster load times is that I *have more time to do the things I love*.

Figure 4-4 shows the relationship between SSD, its rational benefits, and its emotional benefits. We'll build on this example later.

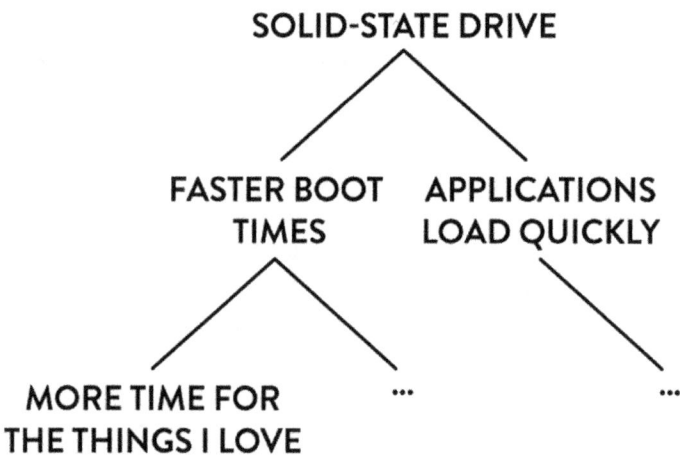

Figure 4-4. A solid-state drive means my laptop boots faster, which gives me more time for the things I love

To summarize, you can see that a solid-state drive means my laptop boots faster, which gives me more times for the things I love. Compared to the simple features-benefits chart, this approach will challenge you to consider your product through the perspective of your audience, which will provide plenty of raw material for your brand execution later.

As you work through the canvas, you'll build a web of features and benefits that will help you connect both rationally and emotionally with your audience.

Building a Ladder of Abstraction

One mental model that's useful when exploring levels of benefits is a concept called the **ladder of abstraction**, which is a concept created by Samuel Ichiye Hayakawa in his book *Language in Thought and Action*.[2]

Hayakawa was a linguist, psychologist, and semanticist, and his thinking gets pretty deep. But the ladder of abstraction will help you orient yourself as you discuss features and different kinds of benefits.

Hayakawa used the ladder to illustrate ways humans use language to classify objects and ideas into categories for easy communication. Consider Bessie the Cow, which is his archetypical object for discussion.

Bessie the Cow stands at the bottom of the ladder of abstraction. Although Bessie is in every way different from other cows on an anatomical level, the abstract idea of "cow" allows us to leave behind all of the differences between all the cows in the world and emphasize their similarities, namely, that they are all cows.

That means we can productively discuss cows without having to explain, before each discussion, which specific configuration of atoms we're talking about.

He then illustrates that as we climb the ladder, the rungs become increasingly abstract. We can talk about "livestock," then "farm assets," and all the way up to the concept of "wealth."

Moving up the ladder answers why questions, such as "Why do I want cattle? To build wealth."

Moving down the ladder allows us to become increasingly concrete, answering the how questions, like "How can we build wealth? By owning cattle." See Figure 4-5.

---

[2] Harvest Original, 1991

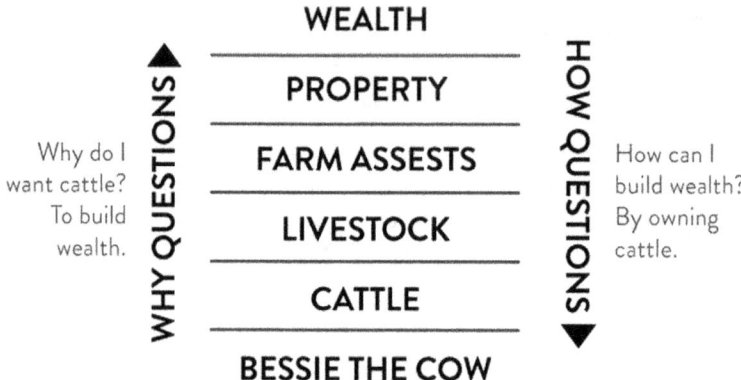

Figure 4-5. Illustration of the ladder of abstraction

In the case of brand strategy, Features answer how questions near the bottom, while emotional benefits answer why questions near the top. Why do I want a solid-state hard drive? To spend more time on things I care about. See Figure 4-6.

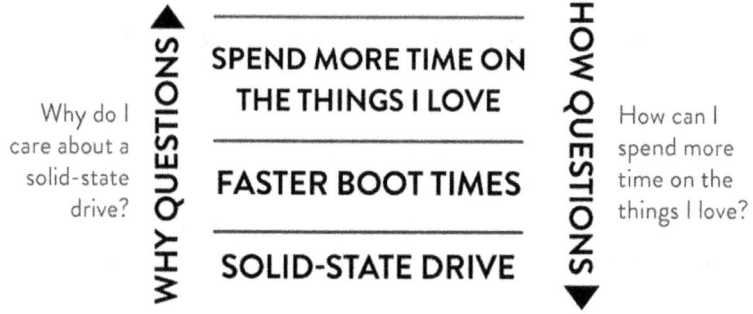

Figure 4-6. Example ladder of abstraction

Balancing Emotions and Facts

A strong and comprehensive brand strategy will include content at all levels of abstraction, combining strong emotion with specific facts. It's important for your strategy to be built on both emotions and facts for a couple of reasons.

First, communications that rely on emotion alone will feel disingenuous or over the top. Think about the late-night infomercials—you know, the ones that feature a mom, in the midst of cooking dinner for a roomful of crazy kids, who reaches into the pantry for a can of corn only to have the pantry's disorganized contents falls all over the floor. And of course, it's all shot in black and white.

Those ads feel like caricatures or parodies—the stuff of gimmicky as-seen-on-TV products and not the domain of enduring brands.

Or consider cologne ads filled with extremely beautiful and rich people running in slow motion across a craggy Mediterranean beach. The implicit message is that this could be your life too, if only you were to buy this fragrance.

Sure, that type of advertising is definitely emotional, but it's also hollow. We just don't believe it. And that's what happens when your strategy is heavily weighted with emotion at the top of the ladder. But there's also danger in stripping all the emotion from your brand and leaning only on rational appeals.

A strong brand will incorporate rational appeals with emotional concepts. If emotion without fact seems vacuous, facts without emotion will come across as just plain boring.

I've seen this issue on many early-stage startup web sites, where the headline on the home page says something like, "An API for search" and nothing more. Again, it's kind of like someone reading you a story's bullet points rather than getting to expense the narrative.

If you climb to the top of a ladder without any support at the bottom, the ladder will become unstable and likely come crashing down, as is the case with emotion-only language. On the other hand, standing on the bottom rung of a ladder is safe, but it also won't take you anywhere. You need both to be effective.

Staying Grounded

Another practical benefit of mapping the features-benefits continuum is that this process will keep you and your team honest and, as we'll see later, more authentic.

One of the most common rookie mistakes founders make is the use of casual superlatives. Superlatives include phrases like "The best way…" or "The fastest way…"

So many home pages make claims like these, and rarely do they back them up with fact. In many ways, these are the worst kinds of emotional claims. Are you really the fastest or easiest? Can the claim even be proven or disproven? Does anyone care?

Superlative claims come across as lazy to the informed observer, but much worse, your audience almost certainly reads right past them.

Chapter 4 | Rational and Emotional Benefits

This kind of messaging doesn't feel authentic, just like it wouldn't feel authentic if a person walked up to you and said, "Hey, I'm the coolest person you'll ever meet." Not only would you not believe them, you probably wouldn't trust anything they said after that and would likely be at least a little creeped out.

As normal humans navigating life, we're constantly bombarded by claims of fastest, cheapest, coolest, and craziest so much that we've developed a kind of blindness to such unfounded assertions.

Rather than pick this low-hanging and likely rotten fruit, do the hard work of connecting your benefits to your features up and down the ladder. This section will show you how.

Rational Benefits

Let's start with rational benefits. Rational benefits are the outcomes of your key features, and they answer the question So what? A user would ask of everything you offer and move a step or two up the ladder of abstraction.

The classic example comes from a quote by Theodore Levitt, famous Harvard professor of economics known for his *Harvard Business Review* article "Marketing Myopia."[3] Levitt said,

> "People don't want to buy a quarter-inch drill. They want a quarter-inch hole."

Levitt here is getting at the rational benefit of a quarter-inch drill bit. The hole is one way a person might experience the use of the bit.

A solid-state hard drive means the computer will boot with lightning speed. A 24-hour store means you can shop whenever you want. Batteries included with that toy? That means no delay in playtime.

In addition to answering the So what? question, rational benefits capture *how your customers experience those features*.

As you think about delivering unique value, one way to differentiate is in your brand's approach to delivering specific outcomes. We'll discuss how that comes to life below.

---

[3] https://hbr.org/2004/07/marketing-myopia

Do the Work for Your Customers

Before we fully unpack rational benefits, we should talk about a major reason this section matters. We've already discussed how rational benefits help set the groundwork for an emotional appeal, but there's another reason to identify the connection between features and rational benefits.

Here's the problem with simply listing features: doing so pushes all the cognitive burden to your audience, leaving it entirely up to them to connect the conceptual dots between your claim and why they should care.

To be sure, your customers aren't stupid. But they *do* have thousands of marketing messages pointed directly at their brains all day every day. That kind of value causes mental fatigue, and it's just not realistic to expect them to make the right connections between your feature list and what it means for them on their own.

You might be thinking, "Well, *my* customers are actually super smart, I don't need to spell it out for them." In reality, this perspective is entirely company-centric, self-centered, and not empathic to the customer reality at all.

Instead of making them do the mental legwork of trying to answer So what? and, even worse, getting the answer wrong, smart brands paint the picture fully by proving clarity on why their offering matters.

Once you've completed this section, your team will have a handy checklist of the primary reasons your product matters to your audience, which will prove useful in all sorts of situations, from conversations with prospects to writing web site copy to recruiting new team members.

Let's explore an example to see what that can look like by turning back to our example company, MailChimp, which we introduced in Chapter 3, and which we'll return to in each following chapter as we complete the Brand Strategy Canvas.

Example Rational Benefits

> *Only need to login to (and remember the password for) one tool; manage all marketing in a single place; total control over your channels, and a cohesive experience across each; simple navigation; find what you need and do more work faster; supportive and empathic interaction design; fast help whenever and however you need it, either self-serve, from us, or from a trusted partner; know how your campaigns are performing across channels*

In the example, you begin to see *how* the customer experiences the features highlighted in the prior box, along with thoughts on why it all matters for the customer.

Chapter 4 | Rational and Emotional Benefits

The result of all those features, the so what, is that I can manage all my marketing in a *single place*, with control and a cohesive experience. As a busy marketer, figuring out how to deal with all the moving parts of a complex operation might feel overwhelming, but into the complexity, Mailchimp has designed *simple* navigation across the various parts.

All of that is made even better through the *empathic* user interface and *simple* navigation across all the different parts. Those benefits probably sound great for our busy target audience. They're sophisticated, but don't have time to master a complex UI, so simplicity is key for them.

Finally, whether they're small business owners or heads of marketing, they will likely need help at some point. The good news for anyone in our audience? There are multiple kinds of support available when I need it, from *trusted* partners.

To reiterate, rational benefits speak to *how* the features are experienced.

As mentioned before, features alone aren't particularly useful for building a lasting brand because anyone can copy them. On top of that, as a startup, how often do the specifics of your feature set change? Probably somewhat frequently.

For those reasons, you really can't build a brand based on features.

You *can*, however, begin to differentiate based on how you articulate the benefits, and that begins here, with rational benefits.

As for counter examples, think about Mailchimp's competition and how they might talk about their benefits. They likely all offer email design tools, but how would they describe them? They're probably not designed empathetically. And if they are, their messaging doesn't bother to communicate them as such.

Overall, the competition may offer similar features in a line-by-line comparison but the way they're delivered—and how customers experience them—couldn't be any different.

In light of the features-benefits continuum, it's important that you don't skip this step. As we discussed, clear rational benefits will provide you with lots of copy points as you develop your web site and other assets, and your team will continue to reference them going forward.

On top of that, rational benefits are the bridge to emotional benefits. Believe me, it's really hard to jump from features all the way to emotional benefits without coming across as either naive or as a huckster, so spend the time here before moving on to emotional benefits, which are coming next.

THOUGHT STARTERS

- What are the tangible benefits of your product?
- How does each feature actually impact your target audience?
- How does each one improve their lives?
- What are the top three most unique rational benefits?

Emotional Benefits

Now you have a solid list of important and differentiated features, along with a several reasons for your audience to care about them. That's a strong foundation for exploring emotional benefits, which are, in my opinion, where things start to get really fun.

Here's why: all the sections up to this point have been largely about observations, like who are my customers, what do they offer them, and what's going on in the market?

With emotional benefits, you start getting into the heads of your customer to reflect on and empathize with how your brand affects them at the deepest levels.

Your insights here are definitely based on those prior observations, but they add in a creative and interpretive layer.

That's challenging and fun, but it's also highly powerful. Most startups don't bother to build emotion into their brands; they stop at rational benefits and often just list features. **That means you'll have plenty of room for powerful storytelling and differentiation.**

So what's the heuristic for this section?

If the main question for rational benefits is "So what?" for emotional benefits, we want to unpack "So that." In other words, **what's the emotional payoff of your offering?**

That probably sounds lofty, so let's look at an example.

Example Emotional Benefits

Peace of mind from using a single tool, instead of learning multiple platforms; delight in the creation process; satisfaction in the quality of the experience; enjoyment of the marketing design process; confidence in my ability to get help when I need it; low stress related to my marketing systems; clarity of purpose

In this example, the fact that Mailchimp includes lots of marketing channels leads to *peace of mind* vs. the stress of having to remember how to use, and pay for, lots of different tools. Customers will experience *delight* through the easy and beautiful interface. Instead of feeling overwhelmed, they'll experience *enjoyment* as they create campaigns.

As you can see, words like "peace of mind," "delight," and "satisfaction" move from the realm of listing features into the world of emotions and carry more meaning as a result. Certainly, these claims are *built* upon the features—otherwise, they wouldn't be authentic.

But by moving beyond bullet points listing what your product does, you can begin to appeal to the emotional parts of your customers' minds, which, as the science tells us, will help ensure your message sticks.

So how do you determine the emotional benefits of your product? There's no single way to get there, but I've picked up a few tactics over the years.

Tactics for Discovering Emotional Benefits

First, remember that it starts with customer empathy, so listen closely in your customer conversations. Ask questions like "How do you feel when you use the product" and "What does this solve for you?"

Most people don't think deeply about their feelings, though, especially as it relates to using SaaS products, so don't expect customers to articulate their deepest needs in flowery language. That means you'll need to listen closely.

Also pay attention to how they characterize the problem they're solving and the *frustrations* that come with it. They might express things like stress about too many priorities, annoyance with unfriendly interfaces, or overwhelm from the number of things on their plate.

Often, your emotional benefits can be found in the opposites of those words. For example, "peace of mind" is a great antidote to the overwhelm and frustration caused by the profusion of marketing tools and platforms, so it may serve is a perfect emotional benefit to explore.

Finally, consider using a list of emotions like the Feelings Inventory[4] to help jumpstart your thinking and connect the dots between what customers describe and a particular feeling.

To stay organized, try using a mind map to connect features to rational benefits to emotional benefits. Having everything in a single view will help you dig into the details while keeping an eye on the big picture.

THOUGHT STARTERS

- What are the intangible benefits of your product?
- What descriptive language do customers use when discussing your product?
- What types of words do they use when describing their problems and frustrations?
- What need or challenge of the target audience does each emotional benefit address?
- Do your emotional benefits clearly connect back to rational benefits and the underlying features?

Bringing It All Together, or a Tale of Two Campaigns

Features, rational benefits, and emotional benefits all provide critical input to your positioning statement, but they can also prove useful later on as you develop campaign concepts and key messaging.

Before we explore how this continuum manifests in the execution of your strategy, let's recap a few examples of the features-benefits continuum.

A quarter-inch drill bit (feature) buys holes in my wall (rational) that I use for hanging paintings by my favorite artist (rational), which instills a sense of pride (emotional) from supporting the local art scene, along with prestige among my friend group (emotional) for being such a savvy consumer.

A solid-state hard drive (feature) makes my laptop boot quickly (rational) and helps applications load two times faster (rational) so that I can finish my work and spend more time with my family (emotional). See Figure 4-7 for an illustration of the relationships between these features and benefits.

---

[4] www.cnvc.org/sites/default/files/feelings_inventory_0.pdf

Chapter 4 | Rational and Emotional Benefits

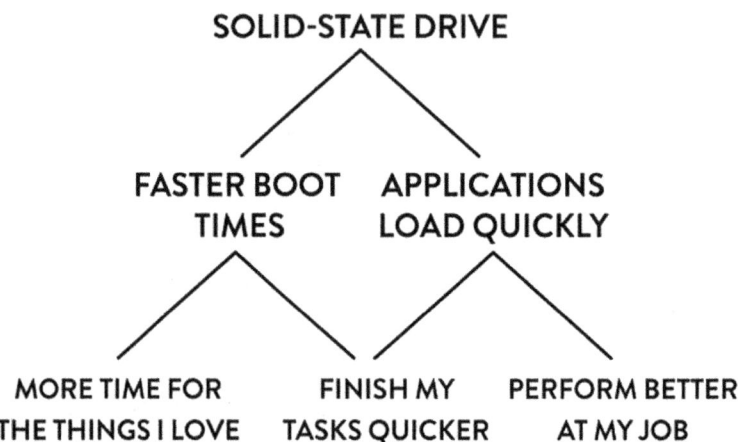

Figure 4-7. Illustrated relationship between features and benefits

A massive inventory of shoes (feature) means that there lots of relevant shoes for me to choose from (rational) leading to peace of mind about my purchase (emotional).

Later, when you're developing web site copy or ad campaigns, **features and benefits become incredibly practical, as they can help inspire the overall big idea while also provide tangible reasons to believe the claim of the campaign.**

While I wouldn't consider these rules hard and fast, I've often seen a mapping of concepts that looks something like this:

- **Emotional benefits**—high-level big idea campaign direction influencing tone, style, and overall direction
- **Rational benefits**—key copy points that flesh out the campaign idea, sometimes subheads or key sections on a web site
- **Features**—the proof points that support the claims made by the rational benefits

Using our laptop example, you could imagine a series of print ads all organized around the theme of the importance of making more time to do the things that you love with your family. That's the big idea stemming from the emotional benefit.

Then each ad in the campaign might explore a different facet of the idea, leading with a single rational benefit per ad, supported by the relevant features.

Taken as a whole, the notion that the laptop brand supports and enables more family time would become clear. As a result, instead of getting lost in the sea of feature comparisons and competition, over time, such a brand would build a position as a brand that empathizes the plight of the working professional with a family.

Once you have a strong understanding of your brand's emotional benefits, all sorts of creative directions will become evident, each one based on the truth of your offering, which come through via your features.

Let's consider another example, using the same baseline information. Going back to our laptop brand, in addition to creating more time to do the things I love, another emotional benefit we might highlight is that the speed of the laptop helps me *perform better at my job*. What would happen if we doubled down to create a campaign focused on that idea?

All the features and benefits are identical to the "time for things I love" direction, but the emotional payoff of performing better is completely different.

In that scenario, it's all about driving value for my team, making my boss look good, standing out from my peers, and delivering results for my company—same features, same rational benefits, completely different approach overall.

So, given the multitude of options available, how do you know which direction to pick?

That depends on the Market Opportunity section of the canvas, your final brand strategy, and your positioning statement, which we'll cover in the next section.

The key here is that that fully exploring all your features and benefits will provide you with an inventory of powerful and authentic ideas for creating a unique position in the market.

Conclusion

On the surface, features and benefits might seem like a straightforward aspect of your product. But hopefully, after working through these exercises, you can see the competitive edge you'll gain by investing in the process. In the end, you and your team will have clarity on how different parts of your product resonate, both cognitively and emotionally, which will serve as a solid foundation for building your brand.

Chapter 4 | Rational and Emotional Benefits

THOUGHT STARTERS

Your main homework for this section is to create a features-benefits continuum of your own. In a blank spreadsheet, add all your features to the first column.

In the second column, add one rational benefit per cell beside each feature. Some features will have multiple benefits, so just add rows to accommodate. Then, add emotional benefits beside each rational benefit.

When you're done, you'll have created a useful reference document for your team to build from.

CHAPTER 5

Brand Positioning

Uncovering the Core of Your Startup Brand Strategy

With a full picture of the relationship between features and benefits, we come now to the centerpiece of the canvas: the positioning statement. It's the geographic center of the canvas but the philosophical center of the strategy process as well.

That's because, as we've said, strategy is, at its heart, a series of choices that define how you'll focus your efforts. With the Brand Strategy Canvas, you've looked broadly outward into the world, then based on your context, added truths to each box that are relevant to your company. You've chosen what to include and what to leave out.

In this chapter, you will review each box you've already completed and then choose the most powerful thoughts from each box. The result is a single sentence that incorporates all of your insights so far. See Figure 5-1.

This positioning statement distills all the research, insight, and context of a strategy into a single sentence that becomes the foundation for your brand execution.

Then, from that sentence, you'll dig deeper to uncover a two- to four-word brand essence that sums up your brand, and all your hard work.

To be sure, this is the most difficult part of the process. After all, you have a lot to say about your company and the world it inhabits, so boiling all that down to a single sentence and a short statement will be tough.

But the good news is that all the work you've done to this point will guide this part of the canvas, because each box you've already completed will serve as a source material for your statement.

Brand Positioning Statement

Must meet all five criteria:
important, unique, believable, actionable, sustainable.

A Audience — For:
Who are they and what is their most important psychographic need or desire as it relates to the brand's category?

B Description — _____ is:
What is the simplest description of the product? Or what is the broader, more strategic frame of reference?

C Benefit — that:
What is the unique, primary benefit or point of difference of the product?

D Proof — because:
What are the factual, meaningful and provable reasons to believe the primary benefit or point of difference?

E Payoff — so that:
What is the ultimate emotional payoff for the customer or user? Does it answer the need in the audience section?

Brand Essence
What is the core idea or defining concept of the brand? Is it tangible or attitudinal? (Unique, succinct, pithy, and ideally 2-4 words.)

Figure 5-1. The positioning statement template

Why a *Statement*?

There's a good chance you've heard of positioning statements, and it's possible you've even read a blog post or two explaining how to write one.

But why is a statement the main artefact of a positioning exercise? Why not a list or a chart or a diagram?

As you invest your time and energy into developing a strategy, at some point, you'll want to actually execute and implement the strategy. That implementation will occur over the course of the life of your company, in web site redesigns and product launches, but also through ongoing and seemingly mundane touchpoints, like transactional emails or support requests.

Founders and executives will have lots of input into the more prominent brand executions, like a new web site or logo. But the frontline employees will have countless opportunities to execute your brand strategy in their daily work. Brands can be built, or destroyed, through the many interactions between a company and its audience.

As we've discussed, it's simply not realistic to expect everyone in your company to remember all of the details from your canvas, and it's even less realistic to expect them to apply all those insights in real time. It's information overload.

That's why a primary goal for the brand strategy process is to provide your team with heuristics to use in their daily planning and work.

You want to make things easy on your team by transforming the deep research and key insights you've conducted and developed so far into a handful of easy-to-apply ideas or heuristics.

For example, when you head to the market to shop for dinner, you don't have to remember every step of each recipe you've planned for the week. Even more, if you've planned well, you don't have to debate with yourself and reconsider your culinary choices as you stand in the aisles, rehashing with yourself or your partner the choice to make chicken instead of fish.

Rather, you just have to recall the key ingredients that constitute each meal that you've chosen ahead of time. In the moment of decision, you just need to focus on what's essential to drive the outcomes you desire.

That's why a positioning *statement* is so handy: it becomes the ingredients list your team can reference whenever they make decisions about your brand.

So how can you make your strategy memorable? Most people have a tough time committing a bulleted list to memory. We're much more likely to recall phrases or sentences.

Because the positioning statement encapsulates your strategy in sentence form, it will be easy for your teams to recall and apply, providing them with all the crucial ingredients of your brand.

As you appreciate by now, this book is about strategy, not execution, so you won't use this statement in your marketing materials. Like most of the canvas, it's an internal tool and a process for sharpening your thinking, challenging assumptions, and making deliberate choices about what matters.

But when it comes time for execution, it will provide you with a short hand for considering your audience and the most important rational and emotional benefits to highlight.

Like the entire canvas, the positioning statement is another powerful heuristic that will help your team execute with quality and consistency.

Positioning Is a Map

There are a few powerful reasons to invest the time and effort needed to craft a positioning statement and brand essence. First, it will serve as the inspiration and guide for your brand strategy, which is an important outcome for your company and team.

As you think about web site copy or the tone and style of your user conference, your positioning statement will clarify your team's thinking and ensure alignment across different parts of the organization. Same ingredients, same recipe.

But as you go to market, your position will play an important customer-facing role as well, as it will also help your *customers* understand where you fit in their understanding of the world.

My favorite metaphor for the concept of positioning is to think of positioning as a map. One use for a map is to help you navigate from point A to point B, which is really important when you know exactly where you currently are and specifically where you want to go.

But what if you're in an unfamiliar area and you're not quite sure where you want to go? Explicit and linear directions don't help so much in that case, which points to the second use for a map: **a map orients its readers to their surroundings.**

I recently planned a trip to Paris, and long before I set foot on its cobblestones, I spent plenty of time with Google Maps understanding the relationships between key landmarks, where the Metro runs, and which neighborhoods have the best places to eat (hint: it turns out it's all of them).

Once we made it to Paris, we used the map to discover things we didn't previously know about, from highly rated boulangeries to small but grandiose medieval churches.

The map was less about tactical navigation and more about *familiarity and context*. It was about understanding where we lived for a couple of weeks.

Now, in some well-known categories, it's possible that customers already know where they are and where they want to go and, as a result, don't rely on maps for orientation. Consumer packaged goods (CPG) products are a typical example of a familiar territory. My bet is that when you run out of toothpaste, you either buy exactly the same brand you've used your entire life or you grab whatever is on sale. It's a simple and low-stakes decision.

I'd also bet that the market your company competes in is newer or more complex than toothpaste. Your buyers may not understand what problem you're solving or even know that such a solution exists and, as a result, don't know how your product should fit into their toolbox. But positioning can help.

For a startup, your positioning orients your audience to the territory you inhabit and tells them specifically how they should think about your brand.

This is important: if you don't tell them, they'll make it up themselves, or worse, your competition will do it for you. Neither of those outcomes is ideal.

In its early days, customer success software maker Gainsight faced exactly this challenge in its effort to provide customer success teams with powerful tools. But at that time, "customer success" was an entirely new concept. Buyers didn't necessarily understand their problem, and they certainly didn't know that something called customer success was the solution.

The market didn't know where Gainsight fit on the map and, as a result, tried to apply imprecise mental models to the company. Gainsight's former CMO, Anthony Kennada, describes early conversations with analysts from Gartner and Forrester:

> So, they said, "You guys are like proactive customer support," or "proactive account management." So, if we didn't create a category, Gainsight would be the proactive account management company, and I think we'd be in a lot different of a place.[1]

---

[1] www.drift.com/blog/gainsight-category-creation/

Chapter 5 | Brand Positioning

Over the past several years, the leadership at Gainsight has positioned the firm as the leader in the customer success category—a category they created through deliberate choices based on their brand strategy.

They were deliberate about this positioning and resisted the market's attempts to describe them in existing terms. They provided a clear map and have built a unicorn as a result.

So is category creation the only reason to invest in positioning? Why do you need to provide a map in the first place? Can't people just connect the dots and figure it all out on their own?

Well, maybe, but "figuring it out" is the wrong framing for this discussion. In reality, your potential customers busy, and they're not going to take the time to figure you out. It's too much work.

Our goal, then, is to provide a clear way for our audience to understand and remember our brand. A good map orients its reader to their surroundings, and over time, the landscape becomes familiar and navigable. We know our favorite route home and where to find our favorite coffee spots. The *patterns* emerge from the previously unfamiliar terrain.

As it turns out, patterns play an important role in brand building. Cognitive psychologists have shown us that brains are pattern-matching machines and that *potentially all brain function* is based on the brain's pattern recognition capabilities.[2]

One outcome of this pattern matching is that we're constantly looking for ways new things relate to concepts we already understand.

Have you ever told a friend about a new book you've just finished reading, and they say something like, "Oh cool that sounds like Harry Potter but with vampires." This happens with new company ideas too: "It's like Uber but for landscapers."

People automatically and subconsciously make these "X-for-Y" analogies whenever they encounter a new object or idea. Your positioning efforts will help ensure those variables are filled with the most powerful and relevant associations, rather than leaving it all to chance and hoping for the best.

Another outcome of our brain's natural pattern-matching tendency is that we have trouble making memories from thoughts and ideas we don't already have a mental map for. If we don't understand the context, it's harder to store in memory.

It turns out some memories are created from various senses, like sight or sound. But there's another type of memory called **semantic encoding** that

---

[2] www.ncbi.nlm.nih.gov/pmc/articles/PMC4141622/

The Brand Strategy Canvas

deals with meaning and context, and it is believed that this is the way long-term memories are stored.[3]

Positioning will help your audience understand *and* remember your offering by providing a clear map to decode and store your context.

To understand how positioning addresses with this realty, let's look to the classic book on the subject, simply called *Positioning,* by Jack Trout and Al Ries. Anyone discussing positioning should start there, and I highly recommend reading the book.

A central premise for positioning, in both *Positioining* and in the practice in general, is this:

> *The mind, as a defense against the volume of today's communications, screens and rejects much of the information offered it. In general, the mind accepts only that which matches prior knowledge or experience.*[4]

People are simply overloaded by communications of all types, and as a survival method, people's brains tune out most new information, processing and accepting information that's consistent with their existing view of the world.

Given this information overload, how can a brand communicate its value to a market in need? According to Ries and Trout, "You look for the solution to your problem not inside the product, not even inside your own mind. You look for the solution to your problem inside the prospect's mind."

In other words, you draw a map that illustrates where your offering fits within the territory they're already familiar with. The work on the canvas so far should provide solid context for this exercise. You've dug into your audience, you know how they perceive the market, and you know what the competition is up to. These perceptions are central to this step of strategy development.

That's because, "the essence of positioning thinking is to accept the perceptions as reality and then restructure those perceptions to create the position you desire."[5]

---

[3] www.ncbi.nlm.nih.gov/pmc/articles/PMC4141622/
[4] Ries, Al, and Jack Trout. *Positioning: The Battle for Your Mind.* New York, NY: McGraw-Hill, 2010.
[5] Ries, Al, and Jack Trout. *Positioning: The Battle for Your Mind.* New York, NY: McGraw-Hill, 2010.

Your map, then, won't draw a foreign and unknown landscape. I love the maps drawn in *The Lord of the Rings* and other fantasy books, but they're not very useful for navigating and understanding the world I actually inhabit.

Instead, your positioning statement will build from the insights you've already gathered in your research so far. The task now is to survey that landscape to craft and idea that will connect to what your audience already believes about the world.

To get started, we'll look at the parts of the positioning statement, then unpack an example and discuss how it all fits together.

First, Table 5-1 shows the parts of the positioning statement.

Table 5-1. Parts of the positioning statement

Audience	Who are they, and what is their most important psychographic need or desire as it relates to the brand's category? Focus on describing a single persona. In other words, don't cram two or more unique audiences into this section; it's all about choice
Brand description	What is the simplest description of the product? Or what is the broader, more strategic frame of reference?
Benefit	What is the unique, primary benefit or point of difference of the product?
Proof	What are the factual, meaningful, and provable reasons to believe the primary benefit or point of difference?
Payoff	What is the ultimate emotional payoff for the customer or user? Does it answer the need in the audience description?
Brand essence	What is the core idea or defining concept of the brand? Is it tangible or attitudinal? (Unique, succinct, pithy, and ideally 2–4 words)

When complete, the statement reads like a sentence:

> *For [**audience**], brand is [**description**] that [**benefit**] because [**proof**] so that [**payoff**].*

Let's jump right into the example to see how this plays out.

Example Positioning Statement

For growing businesses with strong opinions, MailChimp is the creative marketing platform that helps you find your people and keep them engaged because of our comprehensive platform that anyone can use, so that you can be yourself on a bigger stage.

Brand essence: *Keep growing.*

Okay, so we've said a lot about Mailchimp so far, whittling down all the potential directions into a few key insights for each box. Based on what you know about them, you can see how there are tons of potential directions for each phrase in the statement. You'll also see that what you choose for each part of the statement will influence the direction of your strategy overall.

Each decision impacts all others in a complex web, so give yourself some time to explore this section, and try different pieces until the puzzle fits.

To help you get there, let's dig into each line of the example positioning statement and explore how alternative choices would influence the strategy.

Audience

For starters, "growing businesses with strong opinions" (Figure 5-2) represents a specific choice that highlights the attitude of the audience in a manner that's more psychographic than demographic.

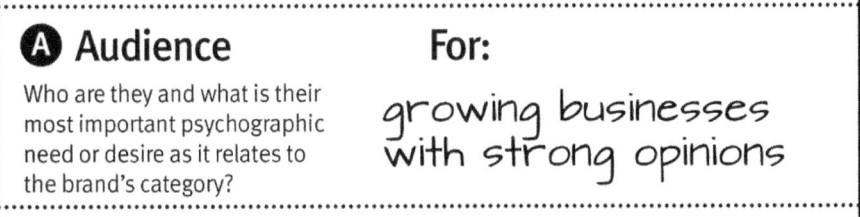

Figure 5-2. The audience description

Though Mailchimp talks a lot about creative businesses, the truth is, if you view yourself as a growing business and have strong belief about the world, Mailchimp is here for you. Plumber, CPA, glass blower—it doesn't matter.

How different would the positioning statement look if it were "For small businesses and nonprofits on a budget" or "for medium-sized businesses with 250 or more employees"?

Chapter 5 | Brand Positioning

That single shift in the language would massively transform the strategic direction. The company might have similar underlying *features*, but you can see how the brand would live on a completely different planet from Mailchimp.

QUICK EXERCISE

One mini-exercise to try in this part of the positioning statement comes from Ries and Trout: "Rather than asking yourself, 'Who are we trying to appeal to?' try asking yourself the opposite question, 'Who should *not* use our brand?'" I call this your anti-audience.

After testing a few iterations of your Audience box, grab a few index cards and try to characterize your anti-audience. For example, a premium coffee roaster might describe its anti-audience as "People who drink coffee only once or twice per month."

This simple little move will help clarify your thinking and draw clear lines around who's in and who's out of your target audience.

The goal of this exercise is to explore and discuss all the edges of your Audience and not to perfectly articulate the anti-audience description, so have fun and push the boundaries a bit.

Brand Description

Next, let's dig into the brand description (Figure 5-3). In the example Description part of the positioning statement, we've described Mailchimp as a "*the creative marketing platform.*" Not just an email or newsletter tool, but a platform that's innately *creative*. This strategic framing will enable more compelling execution later vs. a straightforward descriptor like "newsletter tool."

Figure 5-3. The Product Description

The choice of "creative" works on two levels. First, it speaks to the kind marketing implemented by its users and is a bit of a wink to insiders. "Yeah, we're *creative*, not like those *small* businesses that use Constant Contact." It's a nice signal to current and potential customers, as well as to employees of Mailchimp.

At a higher level, it speaks to the company itself and how it interacts with the world. Everything from the web site's bright colors and quirky illustrations to the type of philanthropic support MailChimp provides reinforces to their audience that "We ourselves are creative, just like you!"

Again, how different would the strategy look if the description were something like "the most powerful email marketing software"? "Email marketing software" draws a hard line around how the company would perceive and talk about itself.

Would the brand really want to focus so specifically on email marketing? It would probably focus our key messages, but it would also limit the scope of our offering to email only.

Instead, "creative marketing platform" is specific enough to manage the scope of the positioning coupled with an emotional differentiator.

Of course, the risk for this part of the statement is to go the opposite direction of "email marketing software" and draw the circle too broadly. To illustrate with an extreme example, what if we'd written "the most powerful business software"? You can see how *business software* goes too up the ladder of abstraction and is too broad to be meaningful to the company or the audience.

So how should you decide between a straightforward description and a more strategic framing? One rule of thumb is to consider the maturity of your category. In other words, are there lots of incumbents, or are you creating a new category?

If you're entering a crowded space, like online marketing tools, a creative and strategic framing might help drive clear differentiation.

On the other hand, if you're the first mover in a new market, a more direct approach might help you clearly plant a flag in the mind of your audience. In their early days, Gainsight worked hard to position themselves as the leading customer success software vendor while also creating the category of "customer success." For that reason, they probably would have chosen a very direct description for their Brand Strategy Canvas, since something broader or more abstract would further cloud the waters of the new market.

Benefit

There are lots of key benefits, but we've chosen to point out that Mailchimp "helps you find your people and keep them engaged" (Figure 5-4). This dual benefit speaks to the comprehensive nature of the platform.

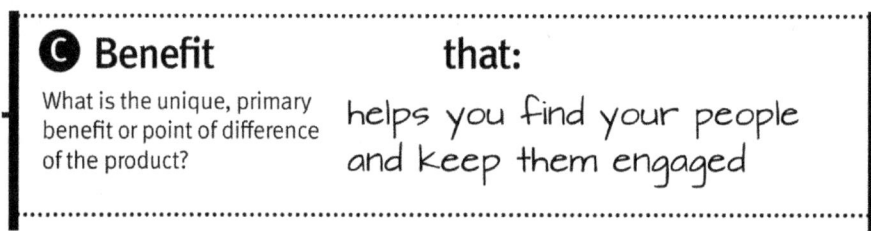

Figure 5-4. Description of the primary benefit

It's not just for blasting emails. Rather, given the list of features, including integrations with advertising platforms and mass mailers, it allows the user to locate their audiences to start a conversation.

For new and existing customers, the platform enables ongoing communication and engagement. And we know these two benefits—both finding new customers and engaging existing ones—are important to growing businesses.

There are many other potential directions for the benefit, given the set of features offered by Mailchimp. We could've emphasized the depth and power of the platform's many features, saying something like, "… that equip teams with customizable tools."

A key benefit like that might speak to an audience of seasoned marketers with experience on other complex marketing platforms, and an overall strategy along those lines would focus more on the power that comes from mastering all the complex features, rather than simplicity and ease of use.

Proof

What's the reason to believe the claim that Mailchimp helps growing businesses find and engage with their audience? It's "because of our comprehensive platform that anyone can use" (Figure 5-5). We know that the tool is built in such a way small business owners can implement even the most complex features themselves, no prior marketing experience required.

The Brand Strategy Canvas

D Proof What are the factual, meaningful and provable reasons to believe the primary benefit or point of difference?	**because:** of our comprehensive platform that anyone can use

Figure 5-5. Description of the main proof point

But that's only true because of the company's investments in intuitive user interfaces, clear design, and thorough help documentation. There are specific product choices we can point to support that claim that the platform is comprehensive and easy to use.

What might alternative approaches to this box look like? This box obviously depends heavily on the prior boxes, so for the sake of illustration, let's say that the prior boxes have emphasized high-end white glove service.

In that case, the Proof box might point out that Mailchimp has invested heavily in building out its partner network and its 24/7 support offering. Those investments would be used as proof points to support claims about, for example, peace of mind for the users, since there's always an expert available to help.

Payoff

Now let's look at that the payoff of the statement, which reads "so that you can be yourself on a bigger stage" (Figure 5-6). The payoff should look back at the audience description and articulate their desires in a succinct and powerful way.

E Payoff What is the ultimate emotional payoff for the customer or user? Does it answer the need in the audience section?	**so that:** you can be yourself on a bigger stage

Figure 5-6. Description of the payoff

We know our audience see themselves as growing companies, with big opinions, and big dreams as well. Mailchimp understands these folks and will help them evolve to bigger and bigger stages.

This aspirational idea pays off what we know about the Audience, namely, that they are "growing businesses with strong opinions." Powerful positioning statements will always possess the kind of logical consistency that comes when Audience and Payoff are closely related.

Once you've completed your positioning statement, one quick way to test its internal consistency is to ask yourself a question like, "Would [audience] care about [payoff]?"

In this case, would a growing business owner with strong opinions care about being herself on a bigger stage? Yep, that makes sense. On the other hand, if the Audience were "small businesses on a budget," this payoff wouldn't resonate, and we should probably reassess part or all of the statement.

To unpack an alternative example of a Proof, what if the rest of the positioning statement was all about concierge service, as we explored in a prior section? If the benefit focused on expert and available care, with proof points about 24/7 service and a robust partner network, what might the payoff look like?

Assuming our customers were busy business owners with many priorities, the payoff might be something like "So that you can focus on running your business." In other words, don't worry about online marketing; you have more important priorities.

Of course, with our current example, a payoff emphasizing the audience's other priorities wouldn't make any sense. That's because we've made deliberate choices in prior boxes of our positioning statement that, to some extent, make the payoff of "you can be yourself on a bigger stage" feel somewhat unsurprising.

And that's a good thing! Aristotle, who wrote extensively about the structure of powerful stories, said story endings should be both unexpected and inevitable. Throughout, the story should provide readers with a clear sense of the what's coming but deliver the ending in a way they couldn't have predicted.

In a crime thriller, you know before sitting down in the theater that the cops will catch the killer. But you don't know *how*, and you'll pay good money to find out.

In a similar way, your positioning statement should lay the inevitable groundwork for the payoff, with the payoff itself delivering a bit of surprise. "Be yourself on a bigger stage" makes perfect sense for this positioning statement, but it's also creative, surprising, and inspirational.

A big part of its energy lies in its emotional nature. The ideal payoff will resonate on a higher emotional level and should build on and transcend the rational benefits already stated. An emotional payoff will inspire and animate your brand in ways that features and rational benefits cannot, and will provide a foothold for differentiation from others in your market. As a result, give this box extra attention as you complete your positioning statement.

Brand Essence

Finally, we come to the Brand Essence. This piece of the positioning statement attempts to distill the defining aspects of your brand into a short statement (Figure 5-7).

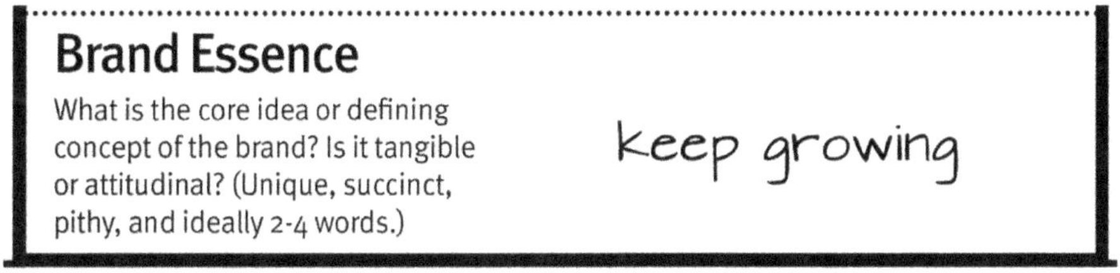

> **Brand Essence**
> What is the core idea or defining concept of the brand? Is it tangible or attitudinal? (Unique, succinct, pithy, and ideally 2-4 words.)
>
> keep growing

Figure 5-7. Articulation of the brand essence

The example Mailchimp strategy covers a lot of ground, including creativity, good taste, design and experience, and a helpful tone, so it's tough to pick just one big idea in 2–3 words.

But for growing business, Mailchimp's efforts all revolve a central idea: keep growing. This idea permeates their choices as the ultimate why at the top of the ladder of abstraction.

Of course, the reasons individual companies or people will want to grow will differ greatly, but the spirit of growth unites them all, and unites the Mailchimp brand strategy.

Because the brand essence is such a powerful part of the strategy process, let's explore a few more aspects of understanding its importance and developing on of your own.

Two Reasons to Develop Your Brand Essence

It's probably clear by now that the trickiest part of your positioning statement is the brand essence. The essence tries to distill your entire canvas into 2–4 words. It's tough, but is it worth the effort? I think so, for two reasons.

First, **editing your thinking this way will challenge you to consider every decision you've made so far**. In the process, you'll challenge your assumptions, often viewing prior choices in a fresh light, and possibly uncover new approaches to reintegrate into prior sections.

In this way, the brand essence serves as kind of a checksum. As technical readers will know, a checksum is a number that allows end users to ensure the veracity of transmitted data. It's basically way for you to assess the contents of the positioning statement and answer the question, "Does this all check out?"

> In the same way, the brand essence ensures the choices in your positioning statement tell a consistent and coherent story.

Practically, if you find yourself struggling with the brand essence, consider reviewing the parts of your positioning statement and making sure they build on each other.

Second, **the essence often inspires interesting ideas for execution**, leading to creative language or taglines that capture the spirit and culture of your company. Constraints breed creativity, and the 2–4-word limit is the ultimate constraint.

In my experience, an effective brand essence will fall into one of two types: rallying cry or promise.

Brand Essence As Rallying Cry

One startup accelerator I worked with had built a reputation for working tirelessly on behalf of their portfolio companies. After lots of thinking, we landed on the brand essence *Never Stop*.

Their strategy was complex, taking into account a half dozen audiences of stakeholders. And yet, the simple notion of Never Stop has become their motto, allowing them to quickly communicate and remind their team about what makes the different from slower-moving organizations competing for similar resources.

Brand Essence As Promise to Uphold

Second, a brand essence can often function as a **promise to uphold**. I once helped rebrand a century-old logistics company that's facing increasing global competition and seeking to reposition itself as an expert boutique firm enabled by smart thinking and creative use of technology.

After spending several weeks diving deep with their team and interviewing their customers, we distilled their brand strategy into a two-word essence: *Uncontained Tenacity*.

As a shipping company, the "uncontained" was a nod to the shipping containers so prevalent in modern logistics, while "tenacity" spoke to the cultural differentiator that team members and customers alike used to describe the company's approach.

Like Never Stop, this essence is aspirational—most great ones are—but it functions more like a promise, between the team and their customers, and among themselves. It's a reminder and encouragement about how the brand behaves that will inform external and internal communication alike.

As you can see, the work to distill your strategy into at 2–4-word statement will take and intellectual rigor, but the resulting clarity and alignment will instill confidence in both your team and your audience.

Generating a Brand Essence

So how do you land on a powerful brand essence? While there are no simple hacks, here's the good news: because you've spent so much time consideration your strategy, my guess is you won't be far off from an essence by the time you need to articulate it.

My primary advice here is to **commit to generating at least 10 different options**. You'll want to stop on the first one and you'll probably be begging to stop after three or four. Your brain will promise you it's perfect, but don't listen. It's just trying to trick you out of the additional hard work.

By committing to at least 10, you're setting the expectation for yourself and your team that you're going to push past the obvious and explore the truly novel. Of course, you may find that your first attempt actually was the best, and that's okay. But at least by then you'll have given yourself the permission to explore.

Reviewing Your Positioning Statement

As you can see, the choices made here will impact future decisions about your brand.

The most important thing to remember about the positioning statement, and brand strategy overall, is that decisions matter.

Given the stakes, I recommend iterating over several versions of your statement. Don't overthink the first few; just get something on paper. Then mix and match different choices and see how they fit together.

Once you complete a version of the statement, use the five criteria in Table 5-2 to assess your statement. Ask yourself, "Is this positing statement…?"

Table 5-2. Criteria for assessing your positioning statement

Important	Will this positioning resonate with the audience? Does it provide a clear "So what?" for their most pressing needs?
Unique	Are you the only company who can make these claims? Is the statement based on differentiated features or ideas?
Believable	Does this statement ring true? Can you back it up with concrete evidence?
Actionable	Does the statement provide you with a clear path to execution? Does it lead naturally to ideas for a brand name, web site design, campaign concepts, and other kinds of execution?
Sustainable	Is the idea big enough to last multiple years, or does it rely on a trend or a fad in the market or in culture?

TIPS FOR EXPOLORING YOUR STATEMENT

I often create a Kanban-style board to explore how different phrasing fits together, allowing me to mix and match different combinations. Many won't really make sense, since many times the parts of the statement are interdependent.

But that's totally okay—we're just exploring at this stage. And many times, the free-form exploration will uncover a combination I hadn't previously considered, opening up an entirely new direction to consider.

Of course, if your style is more hands on, the same approach works with index cards and markers.

Drawing the Right Map

The positioning statement is powerful because it helps clarify and distill all of your potential directions. But there's another reason you'll want to spend plenty of time on this section. As we discussed earlier, *it also provides a frame of reference* for talking about your offering in the context of the market. The map of your territory.

> In other words, a strong position will help people know how your brand fits into the world as your audience knows it.

But drawing a map with the wrong frame of reference can limit your brand's potential, or worse, confuse your audience.

For example, in my hometown of Memphis, there's a wonderful AAA baseball team called the Redbirds. The stadium is legitimately the best in the minors, and it's the only ballpark in America where hotdogs are *not* the best-selling food item (it's actually BBQ nachos, which is amazing as it sounds).

Let's say the Redbirds were working on their positioning statement, and they described themselves as "the top AAA baseball team in Memphis." That claim might be true, but it wouldn't be *useful*, mainly because they're the *only* pro baseball team in the market. They're the best by default.

So in this case, a straightforward positioning is irrelevant and provides no opportunity for further brand development. So how should they position themselves for maximum impact?

For one, drawing a broader map would help, one that takes into account what they've learned about their audience and the competition and the market. In the case of the Redbirds, their competition is not other baseball teams but rather alternative entertainment venues.

The competition is indirect, since the Redbirds are competing for budget and not against a parity offering.

So, a more strategic brand description might look something like "The Memphis Redbirds is the entertainment experience for active families...."

In this way, we've reframed the Redbirds as a purveyor of family-friendly entertainment for busy families who would enjoy the chance to enjoy the outdoors for a few hours, take in a game, have some BBQ nachos, and laugh at the antics between innings.

This framing provides a much richer point of departure for the brand vs. one that describes the brand simply as a AAA baseball team. It's a wholesome and engaging way to spend the afternoon with the family, and it *just happens to be* baseball.

This approach takes into account the desires of their audience as well as the indirect competition from other family fun options, like the zoo or the movies.

With this kind of description, it becomes clear how the strategy will be developed in the context of *all* the options a family has at its disposal. Understanding your framing will also allow you to think in terms of **share of wallet**.

Share of Wallet

When thinking through your positioning and considering various choices, another helpful lens for exploration is to think of how your audience views your offering in the context of *how they allocate their budget*.

In our baseball example, the Redbirds aren't competing against other baseball teams but other family entertainment options, like the Memphis Zoo, the Children's Museum, and other compelling opportunities.

One big question, then, is how we can grab more share of wallet from those in our target audience. If given the choice between, say, the zoo and a day at the ballpark, how can our brand strategy work to increase the likelihood of our audience choosing the latter?

There are lots of answers to that question, but at least one approach is to consider how your self-definition influences your positioning statement, which drives the direction of the entire brand strategy.

In other words, the framing of the Redbirds as a family-focused entertainment experience, rather than a baseball team, provides the platform for competing with the budgetary alternatives.

Often, SaaS startups define themselves in a way that emphasizes the features or functional benefits—the best tool for surveys online, the fastest way to deploy containers, the top baseball team.

As you explore your positioning statement, then, keep in mind how your self-definition will enable you to address the various types of competition.

Conclusion

The positioning statement is the most important part of your brand strategy, so congratulations for making it this far! By this point, you should have several versions of potential statements, as well as a framework for assessing each option.

In the coming chapters, we'll begin exploring ways to bring your strategy to life through execution, but the effectiveness of your execution will depend heavily on the quality of your positioning statement.

I know it feels like a lot of work, but be sure to give yourself and your team plenty of time to ideate and explore. The thinking and effort you invest here will pay off many times over

CHAPTER 6

Defining Your Brand Values

The Basis for What Your Brand Stands For

With the positioning statement in place, we now start exploring how to bring the brand to life. That's right: we're getting closer and closer to execution.

But, as you consider how your brand behaves in the marketplace, it's also important to define the ground truth of your brand's identity. That truth is rooted in your *brand values*, which provide guide rails for what your brand would and wouldn't do and say.

You might say the same thing about people. For example, if you were to think of your brand as a person, how would that person know what's true for them vs. what's out of bounds? What behaviors are consistent with its internal compass? What kinds of language would be true to its identity?

Individual humans face myriad choices every day about where to shop, what to eat, places to go, and people to associate with. For the most thoughtful among us, those choices are based on some combination of personal core values.

© Patrick Woods 2020
P. Woods, *The Brand Strategy Canvas*,
https://doi.org/10.1007/978-1-4842-5159-1_6

A person who values health might choose the kale salad over the chicken and waffles, and someone who values fairness might grab coffee from a shop that pays baristas living wages vs. a minimum wage chain.

Of course, not everyone is so intentional with their decisions and may make choices based on their feelings in the moment, rather than a self-reflection on the things that matter.

Which camp would your brand belong to—the group that deeply considers decisions and opportunities through the lens of well-defined core values or the group that simply makes decisions in the moment?

Which kind of brand do you think has the best chance of telling a consistent story over time?

Brand Values in Action

This talk of values may sound esoteric, but there are many tangible ways your brand values impact real-world decision-making. For example, your brand values will guide the places where you run ad campaigns. Do you care if your ads show up on adult web site or politically polarized news channels? Or, maybe your brand values health, so you decide to advertise at local sporting events.

Your brand values might also affect the kinds of nonprofit organizations your support, as you seek out groups that share similar values to our own.

They'll also influence your brand's stance on social and cultural issues. Consider Nike's decision to make Colin Kaepernick the face of their 2018 "Just Do It" campaign. At the time, NFL star Kaepernick was ostracized by NFL team owners for kneeling during the national anthem and, as a result, became a lightning rod for national discussions of race and political correctness.

In the face of the controversy, Nike leadership doubled down on their support for Kaepernick, running an ad called "Dream Crazy." Though the ad went on to be nominated for an Emmy, the Nike team risked their reputation by entering into such a polarized conversation, but you can bet Nike's brand values guided and informed their discussions at each step of the process.

Finally, brand values can impact the programs and initiatives you promote. Does your brand value education? If so, perhaps you focus on creating in depth content to teach your audience useful skills and create an internship program to recruit and train college grads.

As your brand begins to take on a life of its own, you'll want to work to define your brand values as a guide for your brand's behavior.

> The goal of this section is to deeply consider the list of your brand values so that you'll remain true to those values in your marketing and messaging.

The good news is you've probably already thought about this to some degree, even if implicitly. This step of the process is all about making these values explicit and, perhaps just as important, taking time to discuss with your team.

Vision, Mission, Values

The process of determining your brand values differs from the process of crafting your positionings statement, which was a creative process driven by distilling all of your research into a compelling combination of potential of ideas.

Your values should feel a bit more steadfast. While your positioning statement represents deliberate choices for the sake of taking your company to market, your values shouldn't depend on what's happening in the market nor should they be pulled from thin air.

Rather, **values should result from defining your mission and your vision**. I realize the vocabulary words are starting to pile up, so let's take a step back and explore how the pieces fit together, starting with Table 6-1.

Table 6-1. The relationship between vision, mission, and values

Vision	the future world you want to create
Mission	your company's role in bringing that vision to life
Values	the way you behave toward the world, your customers, and to each other in pursuit of your mission and vision

Your vision of the future should be expansive and likely beyond the reach of your company alone. Your mission should bring to life your specific role in that new world. Your values will provide a litmus test along the way to ensure you remain true to yourself.

I once worked for a machine learning company whose vision was all about a future in which humans and computers would work together, their output together much greater than either on their own. That vision was obviously too big for the company alone to realize, but it helped the team align toward an expansive ideal.

In light of that vision, the mission was to provide world-leading data labeling capabilities to machine learning scientists. There was clear alignment between the mission and the vision. Finally, the company's values provided a framework for delivering that service in a way consistent with the brand and the company.

As you can see, your values tangibly intersect with the world and therefore provide an excellent input into your brand strategy. That said, your values won't be included in any headlines or your company name.

Rather, they're *experienced* by your customers and employees more than they're explicitly promoted. As you'll see in the next section, the other side of the values coin is personality, where things really start to come to life.

Guide to Exploring and Capturing Brand Values

The goal of this section is not to produce a web site–ready list of company value statements. Rather it's to discuss and align on a handful of nouns the will guide how your brand interacts in the world. It's okay if they're not perfect for now, but having the conversation is important.

Why nouns? For one, choosing a single part of speech will focus your team on the idea behind the value, rather than how it's expressed. You'll find your discussion much harder if you have to deal with a blend of nouns, adjectives, adverbs, and phrases.

Also, starting with nouns helps boil down the intention of the value. You can always expand later, but starting with nouns will help your team speak the same language.

EXERCISE

To get started, here's a quick exercise to try. First, start with a list of descriptive nouns (here's a good one: `https://bit.ly/2CFYaA1`). Most people have a hard time just pulling words out of the air, so a list will help you and your team generate ideas for this section.

Have your team write down every one that resonates with them on an index card, one word per card. Do this individually first, rather than as a group discussion.

Next, as a team, start grouping related words. For example, if your list of words has genuineness, candor, and honesty, you'd group those together. This might take a couple tries as you flesh out everyone's input.

Now, with several groups, try to pick the word from each grouping that most clearly and effectively captures and communicates the truth. Move that index card to the top of the list. It's often helpful to take a picture of the groupings for future reference.

If you have more than five or six groups, you might discuss if every value is as meaningful or as important as all the others. You should also make sure each one is distinctive.

But by the end, you should land on a handful of terms that capture what you and, by extension, your brand, believe about the world. Let's turn back to our example to see how the strategy continues to play out.

As you explore your own brand values, let's return to our example brand to see how the Brand Strategy Canvas continues to evolve.

Example of Brand Values

Humility, creativity, independence, community, generosity, weirdness, grit

Now that we're starting to explore how our strategy relates to the world, what are some ways values like these might impact brand strategy?

In this example, Mailchimp values *creativity*. Creativity as a value comes through in their art direction and hand-drawn illustration style, as well as the kinds of companies they feature in their case studies. They include popsicle makers, woodshops, craft breweries, and hand-lettering artists, among others.

Mailchimp has thousands of customers, but on their web site and in case studies, they've chosen to feature businesses with a clear creative bent. In the context of their overall brand strategy, their choice of case studies sends a clear and consistent message about what the company values.

To contrast, what if their success stories revolved around landscaping companies, realtors, and attorneys? I'm sure creativity is important in all of those fields, and I'm positive Mailchimp counts tons of those companies as customers, but from a brand standpoint, you probably wouldn't associate them with the idea of creativity.

Because they value generosity, they might consider employee matching for charitable contributions. A dedication to independence and community, though, might prevent them from sponsoring organizations associated with centralized control and restrictive policies.

Can You See How Brand Values Can Impact Brand Execution?

Consider another example from the world of e-commerce by comparing Zappos.com to luxury retailer Net-a-Porter (`www.net-a-porter.com`).

After exploring their site and reviewing their messaging, one might guess that *frugality* is a Zappos brand value. How would that kind of value come to life?

At the time of this writing, the Zappos site features bright colors, a callout about free shipping and returns, and simple product photos isolated on white backgrounds. It's well-designed but also feels straightforward and no-nonsense.

Net-a-Porter, meanwhile, features rich runway and editorial photography and draws the viewer in with magazine-style sections like "The no-stress dress: Pre-fall's sartorial savior is here" and "Editor's picks: The season's most-wanted new buys and how to style them." Those stylistic choices convey much about the Net-a-Porter brand, but frugality probably isn't one of those things.

To explore further, let's also say that Zappos values *humility*. A brand with such a value would probably be careful about the claims it makes. It would likely avoid superlatives like "The best way to…" or "The world's fastest…"

Finally, consider how your values interact with each other. How would a service-focused brand that's also frugal feel different than a service-focused that values luxury?

Instilling a Sense of Authenticity into Your Brand

As you begin considering ways to bring your brand to life through execution, you should return to your values as a checks and balances for what you're saying and creating.

When your external factors (messaging, design, etc.) align with your internal truths (values), your audience will experience authenticity.

As a result, authenticity is not so much a value as it is the result of consistency between your actions and your beliefs. If a company said they valued creativity but didn't express that in any way, such as highlighting creative customers, you'd probably doubt their claims; they wouldn't feel real.

In my opinion, brands can't claim authenticity any more than they can claim "quality." Some descriptors have to be earned. Just think about your middle school lunch room.

If you stood up and yelled, "Hi friends, I'm really cool. Just trust me!", would anyone actually believe you were cool? Your audience might choose words like crazy, desperate, or delusional—probably everything but what you originally intended.

Conclusion

Compared to more tangible aspects of your brand, like features or benefits, brand values may seem fluffy and inactionable, but clear values will guide your decision-making and ensure your brand acts with consistency. Even better, after working through this section, your team will have clarity on what matters to each of you and to the brand overall.

That set of shared views and beliefs will not only make communication and decision-making faster, it will ensure your brand execution always aligns with the ideals most important to you.

THOUGHT STARTERS
For this section, your main task is to work through the exercise above, discussing and capturing your brand's values.

CHAPTER 7

Creating a Brand Personality

The Process of Bringing Your Brand Strategy to Life

With values in place, we move even closer toward execution. If values are the internal guides of how your brand should interact with the world, your personality helps determine how it's brought to life.

Personality is a concept something we innately understand. We already say things like, "That was the longest coffee date ever. The dude had zero personality" and "She's super inspiring with a magnetic personality." We just get it. And what's great is that innate understanding translates into brands as well.

In people, personality is manifested in things like clothing choices; language; food and drink choices, and other lifestyle and social considerations; and the tone and style of their writing and speech. Usually, those choices communicate something about a person's values and worldview.

And the same is true for brands. Those external choices point to something deeper about what your brand believes about the world.

▪ The goal of this section is to provide your team with clear and colorful descriptions of your brand's personality that will inspire your art and copy.

Meeting Your Brand for a Drink

To develop those colorful descriptions, we'll walk through several exercises. Here's a simple one to get you started: ask what your brand would order at a bar or a coffee shop. This exercise is great because it's quick and relatable and an answer almost immediately comes to mind.

Once, when I facilitated this exercise for one of my brand strategy consulting clients, all five of the stakeholders said their brand would order some type of coffee drink. Some said their brand would take straight double espressos, others said a cappuccino or latte, but one guy was pretty sure the brand would be a fan of Irish Coffee, since the brand works hard and plays hard.

What about your brand? Craft beer? California wine? Fancy cocktail? Or iced coffee?

Now do the same thing with food. If your brand was eating its last meal tonight, what would it order?

Pizza? Surf 'n' turf? Veggie burgers?

Mailchimp actually asked this question to their employees and made a video about it.[1] Answers focused on Tex-Mex and included guacamole, salsa, queso, tacos, and breakfast burritos, along with a few proponents of pizza. Overall, the results were all casual food associated with parties and a good time.

Next, try personifying your brand a little more, and try picturing your brand as a person in your head. Does he have a beard? Glasses? Is she wearing a sundress? Or a pantsuit? Hair up or down? What do they look like when they walk?

Whatever your brand eats, drinks, or looks like, it's less about the actual choice and getting it perfect and more about the social connotations that come along with these things. Images appear in all of our heads at the mention of tiniest personality detail—like a drink at a bar.

---

[1] www.youtube.com/watch?v=1nwwILYYKPY

A woman eating a bone-in ribeye with whiskey vs. a woman eating a mixed green salad with Chardonnay, for instance. You start to know that person, even if just a little.

Of course, there are no wrong answers in exercises like this. What's important is that you and your team have an open and energetic discussion that digs into the underlying assumptions and rationale behind each choice.

In the example, the choices of coffee drinks mattered less than the fact that the team was all roughly in the same conceptual area, and that they all felt similarly about the brand's high energy and work ethic.

What Does Your Brand Believe About the World?

In our next exercise, you'll try to move beyond surface-level approaches to start to give your brand some strong opinions. Drawing on the values you captured in the prior step, and determine what your brand believes about the world, about current events, and about other products.

Strong opinions are generally the clearest opinions. And when you're clear about what you believe, people will understand your personality faster.

And don't be afraid to be polarizing. Strong opinions are inherently controversial. They're also the most convincing. And the people your brand might alienate wouldn't be your customers anyway.

One brand with a strong point of view is, believe or not, a soapmaker called Duke Cannon. Take this example from their FAQ page:

"WILL USING DUKE CANNON SOAP GET ME LAID?

SON, YOU HAVE US CONFUSED WITH A POPULAR BRAND OF SHOWER GELS. THEIR "EFFECT" PROMISES GREATER ATTENTION FROM "EAGER AND ATTRACTIVE YOUNG FEMALES." AND IF YOU BELIEVE THAT LOAD OF BS, YOU ARE A COMPLETE D-BAG. PLEASE LEAVE OUR SITE NOW. OUR SOAP GETS YOU CLEAN, NOT LAID. YOU SHOULD BE ABLE TO TAKE CARE OF THAT YOURSELF."

This example is overflowing with personality, and it's a soap brand, of all things! The language is edgy and direct and takes a clear shot at competitor brand Axe, which, for many years, ran ad campaigns appealing to teenaged males and featured beautiful women falling prey to the "Axe Effect."

Duke Cannon, as a brand, harbors clear and strong beliefs about the world and isn't afraid to put them in writing. Will this approach turn off or potentially offend some people? Definitely. But at the same time, this approach will certainly resonate members of their target audience, engendering a sense of pride, understanding, and brand loyalty.

Strong opinions don't necessarily have to be direct shots at other brands, however. Harlan Estate, for example, is a super high-end exclusive California winery named the "ultimate cult winery" by *The Wine Snob's Dictionary*.[2]

Want to taste some of this coveted wine for yourself? Don't bother with your local wine shop. Before you get the privilege of buying a single bottle (not even a case), you must first join their mailing list and wait your turn. They're not exactly going for conversion rate optimization.

Their wines are listed for thousands of dollars on restaurant menus and on the secondary market, and their brand believes something about wine *and* the world. The brand's beliefs are so strong that that H. William Harlan penned a six-page "letter from the proprietor" that gives background on the family, the land, and the winery. He covers lots of ground, and closes with this statement:

> Yet we have only just begun to understand this land sufficiently to bring it into its current form. And I feel that is as it should be, for fine wines evolve over decades, and winegrowing estates, families, and communities across generations.

Do six-page PDFs with flowery language help sell wine? In the case of Harlan Estate, you bet. Of course, that kind of language will turn a lot of people off. After all, wine is already considered by many to be the realm of wealthy snobs, and letters from proprietors probably don't help that image. But, for some people, these attitudes expressed in this way will resonate.

In Chapter 5 we explored how describing your anti-audience can help focus the definition of our actual audience. I imagine Harlan Estate has a clear understanding of both. They know their audience, and they're not afraid to express their opinions to a group of people who shares them.

The Power of Personality

As you being to explore these exercises, you'll quickly see how a brand with a strong personality is so much more interesting and meaningful than one without.

---

[2] www.vanityfair.com/news/2005/11/winesnob200511

The Duke Cannon web site could say, "the easiest way to get clean" or "the biggest bars of soap online." Harlan Estate could say, "the best wine money can buy."

Those are the easy, obvious positions. The "what" to say without thought about "how" to say it.

But we now know there's more to the story. By fleshing out the personality behind the voice, we feel like we know these brands.

When Duke Cannon gives you the finger, you laugh. When Harlan Estate says something like "Winemakers believe that the land speaks to them of possibilities. A winemaker's goal is to express those possibilities, to capture the best of what the land has to offer," you actually nod your head and say, "Yeah, express them."

That's because in addition to feeling like you know the brand through its personality, it also feels authentic. After spending some time with the Duke Cannon brand, there's a high degree of consistency in terms of design, copy, and overall user experience. In fact, when you make a purchase, your confirmation email comes from intern1@dukecannon.com.

Harlan Estate, at the other end of the aesthetic spectrum, reinforces its personality with minimal design, rich black and white photography, and nearly a dozen multipage PDFs about everything from the vintages to the land to the opinions of the founders.

Authenticity emerges when your voice matches your beliefs, and when your design, copy, and experience work in harmony to communicate the truth about your brand personality.

This is why spelling out your values is important. **Your values keep your personality in check, and keep you from saying things that might be funny or entertaining on the surface but that violate your deeper brand truths.**

Let's now look at how Mailchimp might describe its brand personality.

Example Brand Personality

Quirky, positive, friendly, passionate, empathetic, inspirational

Chapter 7 | Creating a Brand Personality

With those exercises under your belt, you can already imagine how the example personality will influence the brand's execution. In the case of Mailchimp, the use of yellow backgrounds and custom illustrations sets the tone, to be sure, but its personality comes through in many other ways as well, from site copy to photography style to its social media presence.

They even produced a series of shorts called *Taking Stock*, "an original series about the awkward day to day life at a stock photography company."

Small companies don't usually have the budget for custom photography, so choosing stock photos is a necessary evil for anyone designing marketing assets. And anyone that's browsed a stock photo site for more than 30 seconds knows how many cringeworthy stock pics are out there.

These videos are a great way for Mailchimp to illustrate that they understand this pain point, and to do so in playful and quirky way. The *Taking Stock* series is part of a category called "Mailchimp Presents," which is described as "A collection of original content that celebrates the entrepreneurial spirit in creative and relatable ways."

Producing lots of high-quality videos is neither easy nor cheap, but they do represent an excellent vehicle for inspiring your audience with positive messages.

Personality comes through in the product itself as well. One of the most stressful moments for any marketer, no matter how large their mailing list, is clicking Send on a new campaign. What if there's a typo? A broken link? An incorrect offer? Once you hit Send, there's no going back.

For as long as I can remember—and I've been a customer for at least a decade—Mailchimp supports users through this stressful moment with a bit of joy: once you've hit send, you're greeted with an animated monkey sliding up and high-fiving the screen.

It's a little empathetic moment that lets the user know that Mailchimp understands the anxiety of the situation and wants to bring a little quirkiness to lighten the mood.

In isolation, each of these choices might seem like little more than a company trying to be goofy or silly. **But in the context of the overall brand strategy, you can draw a clear line from these decisions back to the brand strategy and the attempt to speak to creative owners of growing businesses.**

Now let's compare these choices with a few of Mailchimp's competitors. Constant Contact appears to adopt a more direct and matter-of-fact personality.

At the time of this writing, their homepage hero section features their logo, an 800 number (believe it or not), and a call to action to sign up. There are no links in the navigation to explore other facts of the brand, indicating a clear focus on conversion.

You can get sense for the personality differences between the two brands in the copy choices as well. Where Mailchimp compels its audience to "Design for the business you want to be," Constant Contact says things like "We're committed to helping small businesses and nonprofits succeed—and to being your trusted partner every step of the way."

The former sounds inspirational and encouraging, while the latter, with emphasis on trust and commitment, might be trying to encourage an audience new to, and potentially skeptical about, email marketing.

It's clear that these brands are speaking in very different vernaculars. Of course, there's nothing wrong with that approach, as long as it's rooted in sound strategy. But as you can see, these choices indicate a personality, and strategy, quite different from Mailchimp's.

Let's look at one more brand personality comparison, this time from the world of commerce, by comparing Zappos to Net-a-Porter.

Let's start with the Zappos home page (www.zappos.com). It's to the point, typically featuring seasonal calls to action. Just below, there are bright illustrations that show two cartoon hands high-fiving and a reminder that "Zappos customers enjoy free shipping, free returns, and 24/7 customer service!"

Note that exclamation point! I believe that punctuation can say a lot about a brand, so wield those marks carefully. In this case, the exclaiming point perfectly aligns with the light-heard and positive personality of the brand.

If you look at their blog,[3] the first post is "This Phone Rep Bonded With a Customer for 10 Hours." Every article on their About Us homepage is tagged either "culture" or "community."

Over on their Instagram feed, we find a bright graphic encouraging us to "stay calm, breathe deep, drink water, it's okay, keep going." How's that for passion and empathy?

By comparison, let's look again at Net-a-Porter (www.net-a-porter.com), who, on their homepage, currently features the cover image from the latest edition of their magazine. It's all about THE LEATHER TRENCH and "How to wear fall's seductive, subversive, and super-chic black leather looks."

There's a live feed titled "Showcasing what the world's most stylish women are buying right now." Aside from the photography, everything's black and white, and there are no links to a blog or social sites.

---

[3] www.zappos.com/beyondthebox/

Their About page is super corporate, opening with

> "Since its launch in June 2000, NET-A-PORTER has established itself as the world's premier luxury fashion destination, offering incredible fashion from over 800 of the world's most coveted designer brands, including Gucci, Chloe, Balenciaga, Saint Laurent, Isabel Marant, Prada, and Stella McCartney, more than 200 specialist beauty brands, and new arrivals on site three times a week."

There's definitely a focus on high fashion, commerce, and conversion. It's all about the product, why it would look great on you, and why you should buy it, now please. That's a big difference from the Zappos focus on community and culture.

Again, these choices aren't wrong—there's no value judgement here. But hopefully by now it's clear that the personality expressed in these design and word choices clearly differentiates from a brand like Zappos.

Conclusion

Hopefully all the time and effort invested in developing your canvas has paid off as you've explored your brand's personality. The exercises and discussions may seem silly at first, but they're crucial to discovering and clarifying the key traits of your brand's execution, which will come to life in your copy and design.

In the next chapter, we'll turn to the Message Map, to explore how a brand's personality interacts with the real world.

THOUGHT STARTERS

- What would your brand order in a coffee shop or bar?
- Would your brand prefer a high-end restaurant, a diner, or fast food? What would they order?
- What does your brand believe about the world? How would it feel about current events and cultural trends?
- What polarizing ideas do your brand harbor?

CHAPTER 8

Drafting Key Messages
Expressing Your Brand Strategy to Your Audience

Every time you sit down to create content for your company, how do you know what to say? What big ideas should you try to communicate to your audience? Without a strategy, you probably haven't actually known how to answer those questions, but that's all about to change.

You've finally made it to the bottom of the canvas, arriving at the most execution-oriented portion of the process: the key messages.

> Defining a few keys messages will help you and your team begin determining what specifically your strategy means for the real world, from web site copy to social posts to press releases and all other communication.

But if key messages are execution-oriented, why do they belong as part of a brand strategy? This handoff from strategic thinking to action and execution will help in two big ways.

© Patrick Woods 2020
P. Woods, *The Brand Strategy Canvas*,
https://doi.org/10.1007/978-1-4842-5159-1_8

First, fleshing out your key messages will help ensure that the strategy you've worked so hard developing will actually be *implemented*. Sadly, I've seen lot of great strategic thinking die in a dusty binder on a bookshelf or end up lost in a maze of Dropbox folders forgotten by time.

Teams invest lots of time and money exploring and researching and discussing, write some stuff on a whiteboard at the company off-site, pat themselves on the back, then go back to business as normal.

But no matter how crisp and insightful your ideas truly are, strategy that isn't implemented isn't really a strategy all. The thinking has to be connected to reality in a way that guides people in the right direction and that they can use every day in their jobs.

That's why we've talked about heuristics all through this book—they're the tools your team will use daily to bring your strategy to life. It's also why the key messages section of the canvas is so important. This section is the point of transformation between thought and action.

Along with your positioning statement, the key messages developed here will become the most-used assets from this process. It's where strategy becomes actionable.

The second reason messaging is included in the Brand Strategy Canvas is because it will provide you with a conceptual guide for what your brand does and does not say and do.

Your message map will become a reference document for your team as you build out your brand. The work you do here will help everyone stay aligned on what's important and ensure that your main messages effectively influence your target audience.

Well-defined key messages help you communicate powerful, differentiated ideas consistently and clearly. In this case, your messaging is powerful and *concentrated*.

Avoiding Brand Dilution

What happens when companies don't take time to distill their key messages? Without key messages, your communication will be the opposite: *diluted*.

Lots of startups suffer from diluted messaging. Since they don't have a clear strategy, they simply make things up as they go along, without any overarching outcome in mind. The result is lots of effort but very little in the way of positive outcomes.

The sad thing is that you'll still do all the same work regardless of whether or not you're following a strategy-backed message map: you still have to write the same web copy, craft the same newsletters, make the same posts on social media, and deliver the same sales pitches.

But without the focus of key messages, your story won't be consistent and self-reinforcing. Over the course of several months, you'll have nothing more than a hodgepodge of loosely related sentences and phrases, rather than a drumbeat of the same powerful messages delivered time and again.

Aspects of Key Messages

Your key messages have two high-level purposes: catalysts and guide posts. At first, these two roles might sound at odds.

One sounds energetic and chaotic, while the other sounds reserved and controlled. But in reality, catalysts and guide posts are complimentary.

Key Messages As a Catalyst

As a catalyst, your key messages will provide you and your team with an inventory of powerful things to say, whether you're crafting a sales deck, writing web site copy, to pitching the media.

Why? Because your key messages are based on your fully fleshed-out strategy. As a result, each of your messages will be

- **Meaningful**—because they're based on your target audience
- **Differentiated**—because you've identified the green space in your competitive landscape
- **Clear**—because you've nailed your emotional and rational benefits
- **Consistent**—because you've crafted a compelling positioning statement that will support each message
- **Authentic**—because you've taken the time to explore and express your values
- **Engaging**—because your personality will shine through

Now, each time your team sits down to create content, they'll have a rich library of messages to build from, and they can execute with the confidence that what they're creating will help move the strategy, and the company, forward.

Key Messages As Guideposts

On the other side of the coin, your key messages will serve as *guideposts* as you begin to scale your brand. As you scale, you'll delegate much of the marketing and communications tasks to other team members, many of whom will be new to the company.

You might also engage with outside contractors to execute various parts of your strategy, perhaps working with a copywriter to craft a few case studies or a PR team to start telling your story in the press.

At this stage, a message map will prove critical to delivering a focused effort. With multiple people writing and designing things, clearly defined key messages will keep everyone consistent and on track.

What Key Messages Are Not

The caveat is that while your key messages span the strategic and tactical aspects of your planning, the purpose of this exercise is not writing copy for specific channels.

In other words, we're not ready to start writing homepage headlines or Facebook ads just yet, though as you'll see, specific copy will flow pretty naturally from your key messages. So what *should* you write at this point?

Key Messages Help Tell a Consistently Powerful Story

In short, **your key messages are the three to five concepts you want to communicate whenever your brand speaks**. That includes things you control, like your web site, social channels, or printed sales materials. But it also includes PR opportunities like interviews or guest blogs.

As an example, Net-a-Porter might have a key message along the lines of

> "Our curated selection includes more than 800 of the world's most desirable brands."

That wouldn't be a great homepage headline, as it doesn't communicate a So what? with any degree of emotional impact. But it could certainly serve as a powerful key message.

Just imagine how the brand might work to communicate and reinforce that key message. First, press releases are useful for delivering consistent messaging, and Net-a-Porter might ensure that every single release supported the key message by including the following phrase in every introductory paragraph: "Net-a-Porter, an online luxury retailer whose selection includes more than 800 of the world's most desirable brands, today announced that…"

For seasonal magazines, they might explore ways this particular key message could be brought to life, for example, through featuring key designers or even printing a spread with a photo from every designer they work with in order to illustrate the scope of their offering.

What if for several years, every piece of messaging led with the idea that they offer "800 of the world's most desirable brands?" You can imagine how its audience might begin integrating this idea into their perception of the Net-a-Porter brand over time.

There are lots of ways to *execute* this concept, but you can see how ideas like "curated," "800," and "most desirable brands" can be repeated across channels to drive home the message.

By referencing key messages in this manner, a brand can ensure that a consistent story is delivered across channels and through time.

The point here is that your team should work through the key messages, based on your *strategy*, then ensure they're implemented as frequently as possible.

Let's now look at the final example of our Brand Strategy Canvas and explore the key messages Mailchimp might choose to communicate.

Example of Key Messages

Built for growing businesses.

The always-on marketing platform.

Culture drives creativity.

Empower the underdog.

Let's make the world better, weirder, and more human.

You'll notice in our example that the key messages aren't all that surprising at this point, and that's a good thing. The whole point of key messages is that they should be built on deliberate strategic decisions in order to bring that strategy to life.

By this point in the book, you should be pretty familiar with the fictitious Mailchimp strategy and the choices made throughout, so the key messages should feel fairly expected.

The same will be true for your own key messages. After wrestling with the canvas, your key messages might not seem super sexy or clever. All you're going for here is a few key concepts you want your team to deliver with consistency.

Once you have a few key messages spelled out, the next step is to solidify each message by listing three of four proof points for each message.

Doing so will not only ensure what you're saying is actually true but help you begin fleshing out the specific talking points associated with each key message. Refer back to your positioning statement and to the features and benefits boxes for source material.

For example, if Mailchimp makes wants to focus on the key message, "Built for growing businesses," what might they include as supporting proof points? See Table 8-1.

Table 8-1. Relating key messages to proof points

Key message	Proof points
Built for growing businesses	• Busy customers can manage all their marketing in a single place
	• Our support team is available around the clock, ready to help customers any day and time
	• Our curated experts directory can help companies that haven't yet hired full marketing teams

As you can see, the claim that Mailchimp is "Built for growing businesses" resonates because it's authentic to the other choices Mailchimp has made in its strategy.

In Chapter 7 on brand personality, we discussed how authenticity comes through when your voice matches your beliefs. Authenticity also emerges when your messaging is rooted in truth about your company and brand. Listing proof points, then, will help ensure your messaging remains honest.

Two Types of Key Messages

I think of two types of key messages. The first type is messages that are already inarguably true about your product or company.

If you survey the Mailchimp's website, blog, social sites, and press materials, you'll feel these themes resonating throughout. They take every opportunity to talk about the power of "growing businesses," and that culture drives creativity.

Another great example of this type of key message can be found with Zappos. One of their key messages is "We are powered by service." That includes their shipping policies but also the ways the spotlight their dedicated staff.

Their site even includes a blog post that touts this vignette: "Zapponian Steven Weinstein is obsessed with making sure Zappos customers are perfectly happy. He's so obsessed, in fact, that he stayed on the line with one customer for a whopping 10 hours and 43 minutes!"[1]

On the homepage, the very top of the site is dedicate to a "Customer Service" dropdown, and their 800 number is listed right beside that link.

They take every opportunity to bring to life the idea of service and do so for the other example values as well.

The second type of messages are those that are somewhat aspirational at the moment but that you want to bring to life.

For example, consider a startup that's experienced solid organic growth on their self-serve plan and are starting to shift their go-to market to be more focused on the enterprise.

Their positioning and messaging have emphasized the ease of getting started on their self-serve plan. But as they've tried to move upmarket, they've received feedback that while their product works well in an enterprise setting, their current positioning doesn't resonate with enterprise buyers. The focus on self-serve in the current messaging creates the impression that the product just isn't enterprise-ready.

In this case, messaging can help close the positioning gap between where the company is today and where they want to go.

In that case, their 3–5 key messages will evolve to reflect aspects of their product and brand that will help as they try to appeal to enterprise buyers.

For example, they might downplay the ease of getting started and the low monthly prices in favor of their track record for customer support, expert onboarding teams, and security-focused features.

Note that aspirational messaging isn't disingenuous—it's all rooted in truth about features and beliefs. Rather, it's about choosing which points to invest in across channels and over time. You should be comfortable with this kind of decision-making and prioritization at this point, after all, since choice is the essence of strategy.

---

[1] www.zappos.com/about/stories/record-call

Staying True to Your Brand Voice

To return to the example of Mailchimp, notice that the ways Mailchimp expresses their messages, including their design and copy choices, are all based on their positioning statement and reflect their personality and values.

> The combination of specific messages coupled with their execution comprises a brand's voice.

For Zappos the key message "We are powered by service" could be executed in many different ways based on positioning and personality. But the way Zappos does it is true to who they are, and it feels authentic.

It's the same with people, in that you somehow can innately sense a person's authenticity. For example, it's hard to put your finger on it, but you *just know* how your friends and family speak. But when someone reads aloud something someone else wrote, it sounds and feels different from when they're speaking naturally in conversation. It's all about voice.

> When your brand delivers messages that are inconsistent with your positioning, personality, or values, it will feel inauthentic and out of voice.

This dissonance will confuse your audience and detract from your goal of delivering a consistent message over time.

What if Net-a-Porter had "We are powered by service" as a key message? It's possible for them to deliver that message in their brand voice.

Given their personality, we might imagine an emphasis on concierge service. They probably wouldn't feature stories about long support calls, however, but would likely emphasize expert and expedient service for busy people who don't have the time to deal with support reps.

But we know that for Zappos, creating mini-case study about a 10-hour phone call, which includes a video testimonial of the customer rep, resonates perfectly with their fun and quirky attitude. In that video, the rep even says "That's what's great about Zappos. The customers become your friends."

It's hard to image a borderline snooty brand like Net-a-Porter focusing their efforts on telling a story like that in such a playful and lighthearted manner, but that's totally okay, since that wouldn't be consistent with their brand voice.

The Talk Like a Human Test

"We're the leading SAAS platform for managing on-demand cloud infrastructure."

Have you ever heard a brand speak that way? Maybe it's on their web sites or what a podcast host reads during the sponsor sections. It's clearly marketing speak, and it's why so many startups sound like startups.

In the real world, humans don't actually talk that way, and if they did, you wouldn't want to spend any time with them. Yet so many brands adopt this titled, inauthentic language, and their audience snoozes right past it.

Here's a secret: great writing sounds like a normal person talking.

It's not flowery or formal. It doesn't try to use long, expensive-sounding words. It's direct and simple.

I worked with a great copywriter once, and though he claims not to remember saying it, he shared some advice one afternoon that I think about to this day. It went something like this:

QUICK EXERCISE

Imagine sitting down at a bar, and there's a stranger sitting there, and as you strike up a conversation, he asks what you do. And you say something like "We're the simplest way to do payroll online." Would you actually say that to a real live person? And if you did, would that person laugh in your face? If so, don't talk like that.

It's that simple. When assessing brand voice, consider whether or not a real person would talk that way. Is your copy direct and clear? Or does it feel artificial, filled with buzz words and superlatives?

Conclusion

As you work on this final phase of the canvas, start observing and taking notes on the messaging produced by four or five brands you think do a great job of messaging, positioning, and branding overall. Are their messages consistent over time? Can you identify the underlying handful of key messaging they're trying to communicate?

Chapter 8 | Drafting Key Messages

At the same time, follow the same process for brands that don't seem as strong. Is their messaging consistent, and can you identify the key messages?

As you iterate on your messaging, keep those examples in mind, and try to apply your observations to your own strategy.

THOUGHT STARTERS

- What are your 3–5 key messages?
- For each key message, what are the tangible proof points that support the claim?
- Do the messages reflect of your company values?
- How can you start expressing these messages in light of your positioning and personality?

CHAPTER 9

Completing Your Canvas

Convert Your Strategy into Execution

Way back in Chapter 1, we talked about the baby pigeon problem, which describes how most branding advice for startups rely on the example of giant companies but don't provide tangible guidance for those of us who are just starting out.

For early-stage founders, the question has always been, "What is the path from your startup's birth to a powerhouse brand?"

After completing a few versions of the canvas, I hope you now have a firmer grasp on the mysteries of branding, and that you see that, at its core, brand strategy boils down to a series of deliberate and informed choices.

▪ That in fact, the process of creating a strategy itself really isn't a mystery at all.

Throughout the canvas, you've researched, explored, and debated countless questions about your startup's brand, converting abstract ideas into heuristics that you and your team can use every day.

© Patrick Woods 2020
P. Woods, *The Brand Strategy Canvas*,
https://doi.org/10.1007/978-1-4842-5159-1_9

What Now?

Now that you Canvas is complete, the process of implementing your brand strategy has only just begun. To help you along your way, I'd like to provide some parting thoughts about how to make your strategy real for your customers and the market.

With a complete Canvas in hand, your question now should be, "How can I ensure my team applies our brand heuristics and implements the strategy with consistency and quality?"

To find out, let's walk through an illustration of how the work you've put into creating your canvas will pay off for your brand and see how the Canvas will influence various aspects of your execution.

Applying Your Strategy

For this example, let's fast forward 3 months from the completion of your strategy creation process. You've recently reviewed your canvas and updated it based on market conditions and recent learnings. The strategy is sound, and your team is executing effectively.

In this scenario, you're prepping for a multichannel campaign to coincide with a new release of your core product.

Product launches are innately complex, and as you think about your launch strategy, several questions come to mind:

- What aspects of this news will resonate with our audience?
- What will we say? How will we say it?
- What communication channels will we invest in?
- What about guest posting and launch partners?
- What are the main rational and emotional benefits will we focus on?
- What will the tone and personality of the campaign sound like?
- What kind of art direction will make sense?

At first blush, this inventory of things to consider might feel overwhelming. Especially considering that you must make countless other decisions about operational details, like timing, resources, and budgets.

The Brand Strategy Canvas

While product launches and new campaigns are always stressful, your investment in the Brand Strategy Canvas means you no longer have to start from scratch when building launch plans.

> Your brand heuristics provide a head start for all design, copy, messaging, and marketing decisions.

Here's what I mean:

As you consider the **audience**, you've already defined the main emotional drivers of the people you're trying to reach. In light of that truth, what should you emphasize in your launch? When you think about what channels will prove most effective for reaching them, consider the most salient aspect that you included in your positioning statement. Now have your team dig into all the places where people like that congregate.

To build **messaging**, turn to your message map. What themes should you focus on? What proof points will make your claims believable?

For copy points, your **features-benefits** continuum will help drive key points for your audience and help you move from bullet points, up Maslow's hierarchy, to emotional resonance.

When you think about tone, voice, and creative direction, think about your **personality**, and use those ideas to guide and inspire you

And of course, at the root of it all, you have, in your **positioning statement**, a single sentence, everything you need to know about your audience, their challenges, and how your brand helps.

See Table 9-1 to explore how tactical executions map to parts of the Canvas.

Table 9-1. The relationships between brand execution and various parts of the brand strategy

When exploring these aspects of execution	Look to these elements of strategy
• Copy tone	Audience
• Distribution channels and tactics	
• Copy points	Features and benefits
• Campaign concepts	
• Idea generation	Positioning statement
• Assessing concepts and materials for impact	
• Ensuring clarity and consistency across materials and channels	
• Copy tone and voice	Personality
• Art direction	

In this way, the brand heuristics you've developed will help you answer key questions about your marketing, even in the context of a complex situation like product launches.

In the face of campaigns and the ongoing work of product and brand building, try not to allow all the moving parts to cause you to lose track of all the details of your strategy.

Putting Your Strategy to Work

Finally, here are several practical ways to put your strategy into the hands and heads of your team.

Make It Accessible

The canvas is great for discussing and iterating, but it can be pretty messy for day-to-day use. I recommend distilling the key insights into a slide deck for quick reference.

For most companies, that includes the positioning statement and key messages, but might also include your audience description. Then, make sure everyone in the company, including contractors, has access.

Stay On-Message

You've spent lots of time pondering and refining your strategy, but the rest of the team probably hasn't. It's up to you to encourage and inspire the team with the specifics of the strategy.

Tangibly, that means frequently bringing your brand strategy to the forefront of conversations.

For example, when discussing content, sales collateral, product copy, or any other customer-facing materials, ask the team how their ideas add to or detract from the strategy.

Eventually, your positioning and messages will feel second nature for everyone, but it will likely take many months before everyone is as familiar with the strategy as the founders.

▪ When it comes to strategy, it's impossible to overcommunicate.

In fact, if you feel like you're repeating yourself too much, that's probably a sign your only just starting to communicate with enough consistency to engrain the key messages in your team.

Revisit Your Materials

If your web site, marketing materials, and in-app messaging were all created prior to distilling your strategy, it's likely that you'll need to bring everything into alignment.

To start, create a content inventory, which is a spreadsheet for listing key assets, like various web pages, social accounts, or printed materials. Then, track their status with tags like "needs updating" or "needs review," and include a date column to track next steps. You might also include a Priority column to track high-value assets.

As you prioritize the outdated materials in your inventory, start with the most-seen assets first, and work your way down the list.

Flesh Out Your Values

Many companies I've worked with hadn't had a rich discussion about their company values prior to discussing the canvas. If that's your situation, I'd encourage a separate session to unpack your values and finalize them.

Review Quarterly

You created your strategy at a specific point in time based on data from inside your company and out in the market. The reality is that those factors can and will change, so it's up to you to periodically review your strategy and update it to reflect changes in the market.

If you need to make updates, take care to work as hard on the updates as you did when you created the strategy in the first place. Ask the hard questions and lean into the discussion.

Good Luck!

With that, you now have the knowledge and tools for crafting a brand strategy that works. It's not always easy, but it's always worth it.

APPENDIX A

Brand Strategy Canvas Template

What follows is a blank Brand Strategy Canvas template. You can also access a digital copy of it from www.apress.com/9781484251584.

Appendix A | Brand Strategy Canvas Template

The Brand Strategy Canvas

CREATED FOR:
CREATED BY:
DATE:
VERSION:

Customer/User Insight ⓐ

Competitive Environment ⓒ

Company/Product Features ⓑ

Rational Benefits ⓒ ⓓ

Brand Positioning Statement
Must meet all five criteria:
Important, unique, believable, actionable, sustainable.

ⓐ Audience — For:

ⓑ Description — _____ is:

ⓒ Benefit — that:

Company Values

Emotional Benefits ⓔ

ⓓ Proof — because:

ⓔ Payoff — so that:

Brand Essence

Brand Personality

Key Messages

Created by Archer Malmo. CC Attribution-NonCommercial 4.0 International.

Index

A
Audience insight, 17, 18

B
Brand drift, 7
Brand personality
  defining, 95
  example, 99–101
  meeting, for drink, 96
  power, 98
  strong opinions, 97, 98
Brand strategy canvas
  blank copy, 15
  creation process, 114
  impact
    benefits, 8, 9
    business strategy, gap, 7, 8
    crowd-centric brand, 7
  ongoing pain, 11, 12
  paid advertising, 10
  personality, 115
  positioning statement, 115
  product-market fit, 10
  putting to work
    accessible making, 116
    company values, 117
    make updates, 117
    stay marketing materials, 117
    stay on message, 116, 117
  shift in audience, 10, 11
  startups, 9
  tactical executions map, 115

Brand values
  authenticity, 92
  brand execution, 91, 92
  brand's behavior, 88
  decision-making, 88
  example, Mailchimp, 91
  explore and capture, 90, 91
  nonprofit organizations, 88
  vision and mission relationship, 89, 90
Budgetary incumbents, 38, 39

C
Click thru rates (CTRs), 8
Company/product features
  common issues, 42
  differentiation, 43
  Mailchimp example, 43, 44
  reasons to believe, 42
Competitive environment
  category, 36, 37
  direct and indirect competitors, 38–40
  emotional aspects, 37
  functional aspects, 37
  Mailchimp, example, 40, 41
Crowdsourcing, 6
Customer discovery, 30
Customers, competition, and product
  competitive environment, 46
  points of differentiation, 45
  positioning statement, 46
  relationships, 45

Index

Customer/user insight
    audience description, 34–36
    audience insights, 32, 33
    customer discovery, 30
    decision-making, 29
    demographic vs. psychographic info, 31, 32

D

Demographic, 31
Direct competitor, 38, 40
Distilling process, 16
Duplicated effort, 7

E

Email marketing, 35, 40, 77
Email service provider (ESP), 39, 40
Emotional benefits, 18, 61, 64
    ask questions, 62
    balancing facts, 56, 57
    example, 62
    features benefits, 52–54
        chart, 52
        rational and emotional benefits, 53
        relationship, 64
        SSD, 54
        superlatives, 57
    feelings Inventory, 63
    mind map, 63

F, G, H

Feature parity, 51
Features page, 50
fMRI, 51
Functional aspects, 37

I, J

Indirect competitors, 38
Inefficient advertising, 8

K

Key messages, 23
    aspects
        catalyst, 105
        guideposts, 106
    avoiding brand dilution, 104
    brand speaks, 106, 107
    example, 107, 108
    relating to proof points, 108
    types
        aspiration at moment, 109
        example, staying true, 110
        product or company, true about, 108
        talk like human test, 111

L

Ladder of abstraction
    example, 56
    humans use language, 55
    illustration, 56

M

Mailchimp, positioning statement
    audience, 75, 76
    benefits, 78
    brand description, 76, 77
    brand essence
        checksum, 82
        generating, 83
        ideas for execution, 82
        promise to uphold, 82
        rallying cry, 82
        strategy process, 81
    payoff
        audience description, 79, 80
        emotional nature, 80
    proof, 78, 79

N, O

Newsletter tool, 76

P

Paid advertising, 10
Positioning, map
    category creation, 72
    central premise, 73
    customer success, 71
    navigation, 71
    patterns, 72

positioning thinking, 73
semantic encoding, 72
Positioning statement, 67
    assessing criteria, 84
    brand essence, 22
    example (see Mailchimp, positioning statement)
    generated ideas, 20, 21
    parts, 74
    right map, 84, 85
    strategy, 69, 70
    template, 20, 68
Price sensitivity, 35
Product-and problem-centric, 32
Psychographic, 30, 31, 34

Q

Quarter-inch drill bit, 63

R

Rational benefits, 18, 19, 64
    example, 58–61
    features benefits, 52–54
        chart, 52
        rational and emotional benefits, 53
        relationship, 64
    SSD, 54
    superlatives, 57
    work for your customers, 59
Reactive Posture, 8

S, T, U

Semantic encoding, 72
Share of Wallet, 86
Solid-state hard drive, 53, 56, 58, 63
Start tips, practices
    act of waiting, 25
    choices, make, 24
    customer discovery, 24
    garbage in and out, 24
    iterate, 26
    multiple audiences, 26
    time-tested methods, 23
    work alone, 24, 25
Strategy, 3
    vs. execution, 5
    good, 3
    guiding policy, 3
    heuristic, 4
    practical level, 6

V, W, X, Y, Z

Values and personality, 22, 23

GPSR Compliance

The European Union's (EU) General Product Safety Regulation (GPSR) is a set of rules that requires consumer products to be safe and our obligations to ensure this.

If you have any concerns about our products, you can contact us on

ProductSafety@springernature.com

In case Publisher is established outside the EU, the EU authorized representative is:

Springer Nature Customer Service Center GmbH
Europaplatz 3
69115 Heidelberg, Germany